Establish an Insider Threat Program Under NISPOM

What the ITPSO, FSO and NISP Contractors Need to Know

Jeffrey W. Bennett ISOC, ISP, SAPPC, SFPC

Establish an Insider Threat Program Under NISPOM

What the ITPSO, FSO and NISP Contractors Need to Know

Jeffrey W. Bennett ISOC, ISP, SAPPC, SFPC

Red Bike Publishing LLC
Huntsville, Alabama

Establish an Insider Threat Program Under NISPOM, What the ITPSO, FSO and NISP Contractors Need to Know

Published by: Red Bike Publishing, LLC
Copyright © 2023 by Red Bike Publishing, Huntsville, Alabama
Published in the United States of America
https://www.nispomcentral.com

Library of Congress Control Number: 2023934725
ISBN: 978-1-936800-46-9

ABOUT THE AUTHOR

Jeffrey W. Bennett, ISOC, ISP, SAPPC, SFPC, has a plenty of government, contractor and security experience. Plus he is board certified to protect classified information. He is a former Army officer who has served in military intelligence, logistics and speaks three languages. He has an MBA from Columbia College and a Masters Degree in Acquisitions and Procurement Management from Webster University. Jeff is a featured speaker in many venues including a presenter at the University of Alabama in Huntsville.

To find out more about the author, visit: https://www.nispomcentral.com

ABOUT RED BIKE PUBLISHING

Mission:

Red Bike Publishing exists to create value for our partners, shareholders and customers by building a business to last. This is what we are dedicated to. As the foremost niche publishing organization, we offer what other publishers cannot; focused delivery of industry publications to enhance the professional's skill levels. We do this by writing and publishing superior fiction, nonfiction, traditional and e-book and providing empowering training resources at affordable prices.

Vision:

Red Bike Publishing will be valued for its one of a kind niche publishing and ability to positively impact our customers.

DEDICATION

This book is dedicated to the men and women of all vocations and walks of life who defend our country and protect our Nation's secrets.

ACKNOWLEDGEMENTS

None of this would have been possible without the loving support of my family. You have so willingly provided encouragement while understanding my need to write this book. The time involved in writing and editing meant burning a lot of midnight oil. Kathleen, Patrick, Claire and Molly, I love you all.

Appreciation to countless Insider Threat Program members and Facility Security Officers (FSO) who choose to remain nameless, but have provided excellent technical editing for this project.

I would also like to thank Shama Patel for her social media support and editing services. You can reach her at Evening Light Designs, LLC at https://www.eveninglightdesigns.com.

DISCLAIMER

I wrote this book to provide practical advice, tools, templates to and provoke though for those who are responsible for the critical Insider Threat Program (ITP) work. I have written this book with the understanding that it will advise and assist, but should not be used as a standalone product. My intention is for the reader to apply to an ITP with the cooperation and approval of any contractual, enthical, legal or other compliance requirements.

All ITP questions and concerns should be pursued with your government agency or Cognizant Security Office. This book is also designed to help the reader draw from experience and suggests ways to establish the ITP. Those who are new to the field can use this as a guide to assist with gathering and applying experience and institutional knowledge.

NOTE TO THE READER

You know how there are many opportunities to work with the government but the guidance is disparate? Well I wrote this book to help contractors under the National Industrial Security Program Operating Manual or 32 CFR Part 117, perform on classified contracts and develop security programs to protect classified information. Establishing the Insider Threat Program is just one important part.

Congratulations on buying this book. You have just taken the first step to improving your understanding of how to establish a compliant insider threat program. Inside you'll discover ideas, templates and tools you need to develop programs to protect classified information from the insider threat. In fact, I want you to read the first few chapters today so that you can get a good foundation that you will be able to apply immediately.

This book goes beyond applying business best practices. It dilutes the myriad of guidance and training to a manageable, but aggressive program. For example, much training and focus is directed to government agencies and recommends solutions for those organizations with deep pockets and resources that small businesses and many defense contractors do not possess.

We also discuss the necessary roles and responsibilities for the insider threat program. For example, I provide recommendations for the practical and efficient designation of the facility security officer and insider threat program senior official. In many defense contractors, the roles one employee may have are many. For larger companies, NISPOM responsibilities and positions are accomplished by a team of cleared employees focused on one mission. However, with small companies these roles are held by a single employee performing many tasks. This book can show you how to assign and share critical insider threat program tasks without becoming overwhelmed.

TABLE OF CONTENTS

INTRODUCTION

After years of establishing working groups with government program offices and defense contractors, establishing security programs that meet NISPOM and information security requirements, and advising government and cleared contractor clients, I've decided to write what I've learned. Additionally, I'd like to include what I've learned from subject matter experts and customer emails.

Establishing an Insider Threat Program for NISP Contractors is written primarily for cleared defense contractors to meet Insider Threat Program requirements under the cognizance of the U.S. Government (Defense Counterintelligence and Security Agency (DCSA)). If your organization is not a cleared defense contractor organization, we recommend that you read this holistically and apply it as it best fits. Some of the application may be perfect for demonstrating due diligence as requirements of other oversight organizations that you may fall under. Keep in mind also that we are working on future insider threat program books for commercial businesses and charity organizations.

How to Use This Book

The 32 CFR Part 117, The National Industrial Security Program Operating Manual (NISPOM) requires cleared defense contractors to establish an Insider Threat Program (ITP) within their organization. Application of this book will assist with protecting classified information from a potential insider threat problem as well as help demonstrate an effective program during government customer and Defense Counterintelligence and Security Agency (DCSA) audits.

This book follows government industry guidance. If you apply the information found in this book, you may demonstrate compliance with prime contractor, government customer and the NISPOM requirements. The NISPOM provides guidelines to cleared defense contractors as well as inspectable requirements. Establishing an Insider Threat Program is one of many.

Read the first four chapters immediately. While reading, please notice that our approach differs significantly from the broad insider threat industry best practices scope. First, this is specifically for Facility Security Officers and Insider Threat Program Senior Officials appointed at cleared defense contractor organizations. It's a narrow scope that focuses on insider threats to classified information. Second, while many in the industry teach and focus solely on the cybersecurity methods to discover, document and resolve insider threat issues, we leverage cybersecurity only as it impacts classified information on networks and not as a sole countermeasure. There are many products and services dedicated to monitoring online activity. While important, it is not the singular solution many others may preach or share on social media or advertising platforms. Finally, we do not encourage the spying on or collection of personal information or digging into an employee's private life. Such activity trends in current discussions and training sessions.

For example, tremendous damage to national security occurs absent of computer system, reliance on computer networks or modern means of communication. Even today, the insider threat can cause significant damage that may not be traceable by cybersecurity efforts. This book moves the focus from employees and general online behavior to the actual required protection of assets and how to determine insider threat activities. This book's recommendations do not include cybersecurity efforts unless classified processing and dissemination occurs and we do not need to obsess on active means to track employee activity.

Current insider threat best practices focus exclusively on monitoring employee behavior against the 13 Adjudicative Criteria as applied to the security clearances (behavior red flags) adjudication. Again, an important approach to leverage, but not an entire solution.

The current recommended practices are time consuming approaches that may take focus away from other easier to apply and more effective solutions. Other recommendations focusing on scrutinizing employees may at the very least make employees feel untrusted and at worst may be unethical or must be heavily coordinated with legal representation. Both best practice sets are symptom based causing the identification of a threat and investigation of behavior before action is taken. Aspects of these best practices should be applied to the ITP, but not as the only solution.

I recommend a new approach and practices that reduce vulnerabilities without negatively impacting the work force. You will learn to be innovative in your approach as well as leverage industry best practices for a more effective ITP. These solutions incorporate a systems-based approach that meets the following criteria:

- Document what needs to be protected
- Establish countermeasures to limit access
- Meet reporting requirements for unauthorized access
- Train the workforce

As you read, consider the application to the type of organization. Specifically, whether or not your organization is a possessing or nonpossessing cleared defense contractor.

- Cleared defense contractors that possess classified information and process classified data on information systems-Entire book applies
- Cleared defense contractors that possess classified information, but do not possess classified data on information systems-All sections apply except classified processing
  - Cleared defense contractors that do not possess classified information-All sections apply except classified processing and classified inventory

The NISPOM is established to protect classified information. While the NISPOM proscribes countermeasures to protect classified information, the mitigations are generally applied to detect, deter and defeat adversaries from easily gaining access to classified information. For the most part, these efforts are directed to protect against intruders, not insiders. For example, there are pages of instructions describing how to establish intruder detection systems and monitor them against attempts to acquire classified information during non-duty hours. There are few countermeasures established exclusively to address the insider threat; it's an afterthought and therefor the emphasis for Facility Security Officers (FSO) to establish an additional program.

The insider threat program training available is also cumbersome. Many times contractors are left to interpret what to do. The training also recommends resources that contractors to not have. For example, Training on DCSA websites recommend getting counterintelligence support which is not readily accessible to contractor organizations. Training also recommends hiring behavioral analysts to analyze the workforce. While these recommendations are helpful, they are untenable for many contractors.

We have put this book together to address a specific insider threat against classified information in possessing cleared contractor facilities. For non-possessing facilities I provide recommendations to partner with possessing organizations who host their employees. I also provide case studies on known spies who have either attempted access or have successfully accessed classified information. These were insiders; trusted employees who sought opportunities to commit espionage. These case studies are woven into the chapters of the book to provide relevant examples to establish an effective insider threat program. While you read this book, look for red flag events from these case studies that you can apply to your insider threat program.

CHAPTER 1 INSIDER THREAT PROGRAMS ARE REQUIRED

Cleared defense contractors are required to establish Insider Threat Programs (ITP) and guidance is provided in 32 CFR Part 117, The National Industrial Security Program Operating Manual (NISPOM). This book recommends leveraging NISPOM requirements and discusses valuable methods for executing the requirements. The value is that as you apply the recommendations, you will have the tools necessary to demonstrate compliance during the Defense Counterintelligence and Security Agency (DCSA) reviews.

The DCSA has oversight responsibility of Department of Defense classified information in the cleared defense contractor's hands. DCSA also provide resources to help cleared contractors initiate and maintain their ITPs. There are many components for the established ITP to address and this book will lead you to successfully implementing your very own ITP.

This book can augment your current ITP by providing suggestions that you can use now to develop your tools, templates and processes to protect classified information under your control and ensure cleared employees understand their requirements. In the back of this book are valuable appendices to get you started with setting up your very own ITP, documenting required information, and focusing working groups on reducing risk of insider threat actions.

Before we begin, I'd like to share a bit about expectations of the ITP. As you read this book and look for ways to implement your ITP, keep in mind that your working plan should address threats and be able to demonstrate compliance. For the Department of Defense contractors, compliance can be measured using a methodology found in the *Self*

Inspection Handbook for NISP Contractors, published through the Defense Counterintelligence and Security Agency (DCSA). Others may have similar methodologies to measure compliance, or you may adapt these to measure your program.

Since the ITP applies to cleared defense contractors, is under the cognizance of DCSA and executed under the FSO, this book recommends ways to reduce the workload of the ITP by leveraging FSO tasks.

ITP History

In the past, NISPOM provided focus on protecting classified information from exploitation by foreign adversaries. These protection measures did include viewing insiders as potential threats, but it was not a focus. Within the last few years, the DoD has been making an effort to highlight the growing problem of insider espionage. Current guidance requires the cleared defense contractors to establish and document their additional efforts to evaluate potential insider threat actors. However, there are no additional focus areas, just the same information packaged in new requirements.

The intent of requiring an ITP is for the government to ensure that classified information is protected with an additional focus on the potential of an employee threat. This ITP application concerns protecting classified information and is geared toward cleared employees (security clearances). NISPOM suggests that the FSO be either the ITPSO or a major player in the ITP. I also recommend that the FSO is appointed as the ITPSO. If the organization wants to increase the scope of the ITP beyond the NISPOM, then the ITPSO could be a different entity but they leverage the FSO tasks and repackage FSO efforts to meet ITP documentation requirements. This may not require extra documentation, but the leveraging of existing efforts for ITP application. If the organization decides to hire or appoint a new ITPSO position, then the ITPSO should heavily leverage the FSO's program. These two positions should work hand in hand.

While writing this book, I tried to identify the need for an insider threat focus. I asked the questions:

- Wasn't the requirement to protect classified information sufficient regardless of which entity is trying to get it?
- What is the missing element that requires the focus on the work force?
- Is it important to identify a threat by country or origin?
- Which is more important, to identify intent or to identify capability?
- Is there a problem with the NISPOM recommendations?

The requirements that qualify an employee as a potential insider threat at a cleared defense contractor are:

- Security clearance
- Non-disclosure agreement (NDA)
- Need to know

I also realized the only measurement the NISPOM, DCSA or anyone can really take is the security clearance award and a signed NDA from each individual. Proving need to know is a bit more obscure and harder to manage from a oversight point of view. With that knowledge I began consulting and teaching my unique approach to the ITP.

CHAPTER 2 GETTING STARTED

As mentioned, cleared defense contractors must designate key management personnel which includes the Insider Threat Program Senior Official (ITPSO) and the Facility Security Officer (FSO). For cleared defense contractors, the FSO is the vital link to a successful ITP. The FSO establishes a security program to protect classified information. The FSO is already applying requirements of NISPOM and DCSA reviews the program. In fact, the DCSA conducts the annual review of cleared defense contractors with the FSO. As a matter of process, the DCSA representative will consider the cleared defense contractor's ITP as part of their review with the FSO. If the ITPSO is not the FSO, the FSO will be a key player in the ITP portion of the review.

FSOs are required to perform self-inspections of their security programs. DCSA will review the self-inspection requirement and results. With this in mind, it is a good idea to download or order a print copy of the *Self-Inspection Handbook for NISP Contractors*.

Compliance can be demonstrated confidently when you can run the inspection checklist and document the answers. While the ITPSO is an appointed position, this book recommends the establishment or charter of an ITP Working Group (ITPWG). The ITPWG can be the entity to accomplish the ITP requirements. The ITPWG should be prepared to answer the following questions from the handbook:

• Has the SMO, appointed a contractor employee or employees, in writing as the facility security officer (FSO) and appoint the same employee or a different employee as the Insider Threat Program senior official (ITPSO)?
• Does your ITPSO ensure compliance with insider threat

requirements established in implementing guidance provided by DCSA?

•   Does your company have procedures to gather, integrate, and report relevant and available information indicative of a potential or actual insider threat?

•   Has the company developed and implemented an Insider Threat Program plan endorsed by the SMO?

•   Do you have a written Insider Threat Program plan that has been self-certified to DCSA as current and implemented?

•   Does your company have reporting procedures for employees, supervisors, or other organizational components to refer relevant insider threat information?

•   Does the Insider Threat Program have procedures for clarifying, resolving, and reporting potential insider threat matters as appropriate?

•   Do Insider Threat Program personnel receive regular, timely access to all relevant and credible information to identify violations, areas of concern, or potential insider threat matters?

•   How is the information provided (manually or electronically)?

•   Are actions taken to address insider threat review findings in a timely manner?

•   Are the ITPSO and personnel performing duties related to insider threat program management trained in accordance with guidance provided by DCSA?

•   Does your company ensure all classified IS users are trained on their responsibilities related to the insider threat program?

This book will continue to use these questions as examples so that by the time you are ready to develop, implement, train or review your ITP, you can proceed with confidence. The ITPSO will do well to leverage and document the FSO tasks.

ITP Considerations

This book provides tools and templates that can be applied above what is required in NISPOM. The tools and templates are not a requirement, they will help your organization meet requirements by demonstrating tailored compliance.

Organizations falling under NISPOM would also benefit greatly from including the International Traffic in Arms Regulation (ITAR), Controlled Unclassified Information (CUI) and other contract based sensitive information into the existing ITP. Though not inspectable now, the NISPOM and DoD requirements indicate a trend toward documenting CUI programs. This will occur soon and including them now will only benefit the user.

We feel organizations who do not fall under NISPOM would benefit greatly from establishing an ITP with similar focus. For those readers who do not fall under the NISPOM, this book will direct you to the answers, resources, tools and templates to easily demonstrate your ITP's success.

ITP DEFINITIONS

For ITP purposes, this book considers the insider to be trusted employees with authorization to access classified information. Trusted employees are valued for their subject matter expertise, skills, relationships, capabilities, and talents. Every organization should strive to hire and maintain the best employees and the most trusted and valued employees. In the same respect, each employee should desire to become a trusted insider. In other words, being a trusted employee is a great quality, something to be pursued.

However, understand that these employees can also contribute a degree of vulnerability that should be assumed in the threat risk equation. These trusted employees have access and authorization to work within our facilities and on our contracts. It is these trusted employees whom you can rely to both strengthen the ITP goals as force multipliers. In rare occasions, they are the ones whom you should develop plans to prevent from committing espionage, sabotage or theft.

When it comes to the ITP, good employees should not be led to feel that they are under suspicion, investigation or other negative action. The ITPWG should treat the program as an active measure to evaluate, reduce risk and protect the company and employees.

The following definitions should be comprehended as they are key to overall understanding of ITP goals, roles, and responsibilities.

Insider

Cleared contractor personnel with authorized access to any government or contractor resource, including personnel, facilities, information, equipment, networks, and systems. The insider has three elements that should be considered.

- Authorized
- Security Clearance
- Need to Know

While insider threat is a negative connotation, it's important that we don't view an insider negatively. We want to be sure that Insider Threat is the issue and not all insiders are threats. For this definition, the insider is a good person until indicators warrant ITP action.

Authorized

The insider is permitted access to work, work product and other sensitive information within the organization. They are employed and have permissions to certain or designated areas, information and items. The authorized person is the insider who can be any employee, vendor, consultant or other person who is trusted and vetted to enter and engage with (at some level) your organization assets and employees.

Security Clearance

The security clearances is a determination by the U.S. Government that a cleared employee or cleared defense contractor is trustworthy. Those who hold a security clearance are authorized to access classified information at the same level or below their security clearance level. While the military, DoD civilian employees, and cleared defense contractors may have these security clearances, other organizations may vet information in a similar manner. For example, some non defense organizations may classify their information as proprietary, intellectual property or other company sensitive designation. For the purposes of this book, accessing sensitive information makes a good argument that someone is a trusted insider.

Need to Know

Need to know is a justification that a person is provided authorized access to information. The justification can come in many forms, contract, job description, personal vetting, or level of material contribution. Need to know is a qualifier for access to classification. However, a good practice is to apply need to know regardless of sensitivity. Anyone accessing any information should have a need to know of that information. When we were young and someone was nosy about private discussions, we would say, "none of your business". However, as we get older, we become more polite and maybe more vulnerable.

As long as someone can vet or rationalize providing access, that person is deemed with need to know. However, in professional application we recommend focusing on material contribution. This simply means, what level of work is an individual responsible for.

For example, a human resources employee will have material contribution in the onboarding of employee information and should have access to information to do their job. An engineer will have material contribution to a weapon system development and should be able to view drawings, documents and test results of the specific system. These two should not be sharing their material with each other. Additionally, two engineers in the same company, but working on separate projects, should not be sharing their material with each other.

Need to know should be applied at any organization and not just the cleared defense contractors. For example, personal information should be protected and used by human resources and need to know enforced. Lab experiments or studies should be protected, accessed by the research teams and need to know enforced so that others can't gain access.

Insider Threat

The likelihood, risk, or potential that an insider will use his or her authorized access, wittingly or unwittingly, to do harm to the national security of the United States.

Because of the authorized access to classified information, an insider can cause accidental and malicious damage to national security that may not otherwise be easily detected. An insider may not have access to everything, but what they can access for work, they can also access for harm. What they can't access may be easily obtainable by relationships with other employees.

Intent

This is the motivation of the individual to conduct insider threat activities. They may have several reasons for their actions, but in the end, their actions could cause harm. These reasons could be revenge, unhappy with the organization, adventure, ideology, or something else.

Intent could also be an act of crime, negligence or accidental. The employee may not be an adversary for any other reason as they forget procedures, make a mistake with protocol, or are nonchalant about internal practices.

Sensitive Information

Items and information that if exploited could negatively impact the organization. Sensitive information is a vulnerability that the insider threat program should address. Sensitive information at a defense contractor location may include more specifically items owned by or produced for the government which includes the following items with protection requirements:

- Controlled Technical Information (CTI)
- Classified (National Industrial Security Program Operating Manual (NISPOM))
- Export Controlled (International Traffic In Arms Regulation (ITAR))
- Controlled Unclassified Information (CUI)

It is up to the organization to identify the above sensitive information, mark it, and protect it according to customer requirements Additionally, organizations, including those who are not defense contractors, should identify and mark other protected information such as:
- Customer property
- Intellectual property
- Proprietary
- Personal
- High dollar value
- Financial
- Anything else that loss would require protection measures to mitigate the loss

CHAPTER 3 INSIDER THREAT PROGRAM PURPOSE

The ITP should be designed to deny, detect, deter and report insider threat actions to classified information and demonstrate compliance. The insider threat should be applied as a vulnerability issue to be reduced through risk management efforts. We will get more into how to implement later.

MEASURING RISK

Risk is the calculation of impact of event and vulnerability of sensitive item. There are many ways to measure risk. You may be aware of many yourself. I like to teach the risk equation of vulnerability + sensitive item = risk. With this methodology, we do not have to create complicated algorithms or have difficult discussions about theory. This is a head on approach to addressing the issue of what can someone get to and how can they get to it.

This methodology is beneficial as we do not have to name individuals, research adversarial companies or countries, or undergo many, many working group hours defining specific actions. The methodology I teach also does not involve creating an environment where employees feel untrusted or spied upon. This methodology meets the ITP intent, creates organizational effort, and cooperation.

Why I don't teach adding intent or a specific threat to the equation. Fretting over specific person, country or other details is unnecessary and cumbersome work. Why spend so much time when you can mitigate risk without even needing threat information? So, the question is, why do I care who wants the information or why they are trying to get to it? I already understand that stealing technology is beneficial and it really doesn't matter whether Company A, Country B or Person C is trying to get to it. I just need to understand the information is desirable and that others want it.

While others search for specific threats while observing employee behavior, my process focuses on limiting access and reporting unauthorized attempts to access it. The amount of effort it takes to do research and the lack of actionable information available from the research may not be worth the time, effort and resources. This pulls very valuable ITP resources away from its primary task.

For the ITP, it may be enough to know someone wants the information and can benefit from it. Removing intent and threat from the risk equation, the ITP can focus on what is vulnerable, what vulnerabilities may be and where should we prioritize our efforts to be more effective.

Benefits of an Effective ITP

The insider is a trusted individual who has access to sensitive information. An outsider who does not have access to the desired information has a few choices. They can break in, hack, spy, or take other invasive and detectable means to secure the information they need. These methods are often easily detectable and at a higher risk to the perpetrator.

However, another potentially lucrative option is to recruit a trusted employee to do their work for them. This work can include theft, sabotage, copy, or transmit information, often in hard to detect methods and at more risk to the victim. Many times, trusted employees are successful because this behavior is unexpected of them. The level of trust usually means that these crimes are not noticed until it is far too late. However, an active ITP can reduce the risk to the organization.

Insider Threat Impact and Risk

An insider threat event can have a negative impact on national security and industry resulting in loss of:
- Classified, export-controlled, or proprietary information
- Technological superiority
- Economic advantage

- Warfighter

The idea that a trusted employee, friend or co-worker would conduct such activity is difficult to imagine. Where do you start? and who do you start with? are some questions you might have. Additionally, indications of such activity may be more difficult to find than more obvious thefts or damage events. It can take months or years to discover some activity. However, there are actions ITPWGs can take to become more aware of insider threat activity that can make such incidents more recognizable and actionable.

Research and development organizations, defense contractors, colleges and universities may have facility and personnel security clearances. They may also possess Controlled Technical Information, Controlled Unclassified Information (CUI), classified and International Traffic in Arms (ITAR) controlled information. Information is vulnerable in the insider's hands and can be stolen, given away, released through patents, presentations, and business transactions.

Insiders with access to such information possess potential cutting-edge technologies, solutions, products and services that keep their organizations competitive. This knowledge can also create huge vulnerabilities that an adversary can exploit. Why, If an adversary can take a short cut through a cleared employee, they do not have to put in the level of development work. A viable solution is available if they can get their hands on it.

A proactive ITP can mitigate these risks by identifying all sensitive information, documenting where they exist, marking it, conducting a risk assessment, assigning countermeasures, and measuring effectiveness. The application of the ITP and their activities can positively impact the organization and demonstrate compliance with requirements.

Take note while reading these case studies and applying lessons learned. In these examples, the insider threat actor may have desired to share classified information they have had access to. They contacted foreign actors and offered their services. However, the foreign actors may direct efforts to gain access to additional information they may NOT have access to. This typically means that your insider threat program must establish red flag events. These should trigger when an insider either accesses classified information they are authorized to access, or attempts to access classified information they may not have access to. I will explain further in the following chapters.

ITP Use Cases

Let's look at a few use cases that demonstrate how espionage has occurred and some lessons learned from the events. Consider the elements of recruiting, trusted employee response, employee reporting, enforcement (or lack thereof) of need to know and access to classified information. As you read the cases, think about these elements of each event and form an opinion and an action plan to train your employees to recognize insider threat activities and how they would report them.

In three of these cases, actual classified information removed in a manner controlled by an investigation; in one case it was removed without anyone's knowledge. In three cases diligent employees alerted of unusual occurrences, in the final case, nothing triggered an insider threat reporting event. These cases are summaries of actual documents from the Department of Justice website.

Use Case 1

John Murray Rowe Jr., attempted to provide classified information to the Russian government. Rowe was employed for nearly 40 years as a test engineer for multiple cleared defense contractors and held a TOP SECRET security clearance. Rowe committed a number of security violations and revealed interest in obtaining a security clearance from the Russian government. He was identified as a potential insider threat and terminated from employment.

Based on his conduct, the FBI began an undercover operation to determine Rowe's willingness to communicate classified information to a foreign government. Rowe met with an undercover FBI employee who posed as an agent of the Russian government. Over the course of the next eight months, Rowe exchanged over 300 emails with the purported Russian agent, confirming his willingness to work for the Russian government and discussing his knowledge of classified information relating to U.S. national security and military interests. In one email, Rowe explained, "If I can't get a job here then I'll go work for the other team." In another email, Rowe disclosed national defense information classified as SECRET that concerned specific operating details of the electronic countermeasure systems used by U.S. military fighter jets.

Rowe is charged with attempting to communicate national defense information to aid a foreign government.

The good news is that the co-workers and FSO were diligent and performed their jobs well. NISPOM mandated reporting topics triggered the proper response on three points:

1. The FSO informed DSS that in one of Rowe's social media posts, he stated that he had revealed information regarding U.S. military fighter jets to a woman he thought might be a Russian spy.

2. Rowe attempted to bring a thumb drive into a classified space.

However, he was stopped by a fellow employee who observed him carrying the thumb drive.

3. Rowe inquired about the possibility of simultaneously holding a U.S. security clearance and a Russian security clearance. ROWE was informed that would violate security measures and, thus, was not permitted.

In this case, reporting led to Rowe's termination. However, Rowe still had knowledge of classified information. He continued to provide classified information from memory typed up in emails. Though there is no way to monitor this with a terminated employee, the FSO's training and reporting from other employees worked. Rowe passed classified information to an FBI agent posing as a spy.

Classified information was exchanged via email, but it was head knowledge.
https://www.justice.gov/opa/pr/former-defense-contractor-arrested-attempted-espionage

Use Case 2

Ron Rockwell Hansen, a former Defense Intelligence Agency (DIA) officer, pleaded guilty in connection with his attempted transmission of national defense information to the People's Republic of China. The DIA hired Hansen as a civilian intelligence case officer. While employed, he held a Top Secret clearance.

Agents of a Chinese intelligence service targeted Hansen for recruitment and he began meeting with them regularly, in China. The agents directed to Hansen, the type of information that they were interested in receiving. For his efforts, Hansen received hundreds of thousands of dollars.

Hansen requested specific information from DIA colleagues and recommended collection and transmission techniques to evade detection. The employee reported Hansen's conduct to the DIA and agreed to work with the FBI.

Hansen met with the DIA case officer and was provided the classified information that he requested. The documents Hansen received were classified. Hansen reviewed the documents, asked questions and took notes.

Some points highlighted below should be discussed and addressed by an organization standing up an ITP.

1. The Chinese agents directed the collection of certain information. The cleared employee was not just sharing what they knew, but requesting access to classified information that they had no need to know. That meant that Hansen had to also recruit other cleared employees.

2. Hansen did not remove classified information. He requested classified information from another cleared employee. This is a lesson to be diligent with enforcing need to know. A less aware employee might overlook such a request and enable an insider threat event. In this case, the employee reported the event.

3. Hansen did not take away classified information. Hansen studied, asked questions and ensured he understood the data. He then memorized what he needed to know and walked out with notes and a head full of secrets. Again, good reporting prevented the loss of classified information.

https://www.justice.gov/opa/pr/former-defense-intelligence-officer-pleads-guilty-attempted-espionage

Use Case 3

Robert Patrick Hoffman II was as Cryptologic Technician - Technical (CTT) in the U.S. Navy working with submarines for much of his career. He held security clearances and regularly received access to classified information about submarines and their capabilities including missions, equipment and intelligence.

For unspecified reasons, the FBI initiated an investigation to determine if Hoffman was willing to act as an agent for a foreign government and commit espionage against the United States by divulging classified information. Posing as Russian intelligence, the FBI contacted Hoffman who stated that he was looking forward to "renewing [a] friendship" and was "willing to develop a mutual trust,". He stated that he wanted job assistance and payment as compensation for his activities. He also suggested they communicate by physical, rather than unsecure electronic means.

Eventually Hoffman provided encrypted thumb drives containing classified information at the levels of secret and top secret/sensitive compartmented information. Following these disclosures, FBI and NCIS agents arrested Hoffman.

Some points highlighted below should be discussed and addressed by an organization standing up an ITP.

1.   The FBI set up an operation to see if Hoffman would provide classified information. This would allude to the fact that something was reported about Hoffman that triggered the response. An active and thriving incidence response and reporting process is key to a successful ITP.

2.   While we don't know how Hoffman removed the classified information, we can be assured that it was monitored and tracked. In this case, while classified information was removed and provided by an insider, it was provided to FBI agents posing as

Russian agents. However, the IPTWG would do well to develop methods to discovered when classified information is accessed and attempts to remove it or download it to a recording device (thumb drive) are made. Keep in mind, that such transactions may be authorized, but attempts to bypass authorized methods or gain access to information outside of need to know should be reported.

https://www.justice.gov/opa/pr/former-sailor-sentenced-30-years-prison-attempted-espionage

Use Case 4

Brian Patrick Regan is a 20-year veteran of the United States Air Force, and had been assigned to the Air Force Intelligence Support Group at the Pentagon as well as to the headquarters of the National Reconnaissance Office. He also had racked up more than $100,000 in credit card debt.

At some point late in his career, Regan drafted to Iraqi President Saddam Hussein, Regan wrote, "I am willing to commit espionage against the United States by providing your country with highly classified information. I have a top secret clearance and have access to documents from all of the U.S. intelligence agencies," the quote is from his indictment.

The indictment further claims that Regan demanded $13 million rationalizing that, "If I am caught, I will be imprisoned for the rest of my life, if not executed, for this deed. Considering the risk I am about to take, I will require a minimum payment of $13 million U.S. dollars. There are many people, from movie stars to athletes in the U.S., who receive tens of millions of dollars a year for their trivial contributions. If I'm going to risk my life and the future of my family, I am going to get paid a fair price".

Regan offered to reveal top secret information that directly concerns satellites, early-warning systems, means of defense against large-scale attack, communication intelligence information and major elements of defense strategy.

If that were not enough to convince that insiders are persistent, he also wrote a letter to Muammar Qadhafi of Libya. Regan offered Qadhafi top secret SCI information that directly concerned satellites, early-warning systems, means of defense against large-scale attack, communications intelligence information and major elements of defense strategy.

The indictment states that Regan made a regular practice of accessing IntelLink, the intelligence community's classified Internet. While on the site, he viewed classified information relating to military facilities in Iraq, Iran, Libya, and the People's Republic of China, as well as classified documents relating to current U.S. Intelligence collection capabilities against those countries. This information was not related to his official duties or training.

The FBI began an investigation after an informant from the Libyan Consulate in New York handed the FBI a series of letters from Regan. At the time of his arrest, Regan carried information about the location of classified documents including what he had accessed on IntelLink. One was a recent view of a mobile surface-to-air missile launch facility in the Northern No-Fly Zone in Iraq, and the other was a recent view of a surface-to-surface missile facility in the People's Republic of China.

Some points highlighted below should be discussed and addressed by an organization standing up an ITP.

1.   It was a tip from an informant that led to an investigation and not from a diligent worker. This highlights the importance of an insider threat program, enforcing need to know, training employees to recognize and report suspicious behavior.

2. Need to know was not enforced. This is evidenced in the fact that Regan used IntelLink to access classified information outside of his work scope as stated in the indictment, "This information was not related to his official duties or training."

3. Additionally, Regan removed boxes of classified information from his work location. Think about that. In an environment where classified information should be accounted for, it walked out undetected. Again, a tip was provided from a source outside of the organization

https://www.justice.gov/archive/dag/speeches/2002/021402newsconfere
ncesupercedingindictmentofregan.htm

CHAPTER 4 PRELIMINARY ACTIVITIES

Before we get to the details of the ITP, there are a few preliminary requirements. Many of you may already be established defense contractor entities with employees on-
sight. Some of you may be just getting started and need the following information.

DOCUMENTING THE INSIDER THREAT PROGRAM

As discussed earlier, answering questions from the Self-Inspection Handbook for NISP Contractors helps focus on requirements. The following question applies:

Has the SMO, appointed a contractor employee or employees, in writing as the facility security officer (FSO) and appoint the same employee or a different employee as the Insider Threat Program senior official (ITPSO)?

This is one of the easier questions that can be answered with appointment documentation. Existing defense contractors have already filed with SAM.gov and established themselves as an organization eligible to do business with the U.S. government or other defense contractors. Some of the requirements have included getting the Contractor and Government Entity or CAGE Code, identifying the type of business format, assigning key personnel, and other required filings.

However, to become a cleared defense contractor (a facility clearance) eligible to conduct classified work, there is much more to file in addition to what is required to become a defense contractor.

This includes appointing senior management officials. These security officials are key to the Insider Threat Program's construct. Cleared defense contractors must appoint the following:

- Senior Management Official
- Facility Security Officer
- Insider Threat Program Senior Official

The appointment memorandums in the appendices can constitute artifacts for submittal to DCSA review. See Appendix A for appointment memorandum templates. Appoint these positions in memorandums and have available for audit or review purposes. For more information about security clearances, becoming a cleared defense contractor or performing on classified contracts, see our books and training information available at the end of this book.

GOVERNMENT OVERSIGHT

For the Department of Defense, the Cognizant Security Office is the Defense Counterintelligence and Security Agency (DCSA). The ITP functions and documentation are inspectable items during annual reviews that DCSA performs on cleared defense contractors who possess classified information. However, this requirement may soon roll down to uncleared contractors who possess controlled unclassified information (CUI). If you are not part of the defense industry, it's possible some of your security or quality control requirements are similar.

The DCSA assists, advises and performs oversight functions for the defense contractor. This function includes ensuring the appointment of:

- Senior Management Official
- FSO
- Insider Threat Protection Official

CHAPTER 5 ALL CLEARED DEFENSE CONTRACTORS

A possessing facility is one that has classified information at their location; classified work is performed on-site. A non-possessing facility is one where cleared employees perform classified work at another location. All cleared defense contractors, regardless of possessing or non-possessing classified material on-site, must establish an Insider Threat Program. While possessing facilities with classified information on-site, and those who have additional classified processing requirements have more specific tasks, some ITP tasks are foundational for all facilities.

In general, ITP requirements consist of three topics. First, establish your ITP with the capability to gather, integrate, review, assess, and respond to information derived from a variety of sources. Next, establish procedures for insider threat response actions to both clarify and resolve insider threat matters and to ensure that such response actions are managed by the ITP. Finally, develop procedures to document insider threat matters reported to the ITP and the response actions taken. Execution will depend on how the CDC is organized.

THE NISPOM

This book will help you focus on the fundamentals that lead to ITP success. There are a few simple applications that when employed, will ensure your ITP is considered favorable and performs successfully. We will use the Department Of Defense NISPOM requirements as a baseline for protecting classified information. However, you might be surprised to find that NISPOM does not provide the adequate protection to deter an insider threat. This will be discussed later, but first an introduction to NISPOM.

The NISPOM is guidance provided to cleared defense contractors but can be used for non-DoD organizations as they are good practices and are measurable. The cleared defense contractor requirements found in NISPOM are:

- Implement an Insider Threat Plan (ITP) to deter and detect suspicious activities or threats
- Designate a ITP Senior Official (ITPSO)
- Train the designated ITPSO, ITP group members and all cleared employees
- Implement classified networks monitoring
- Maintain ITP records
- Conduct self-inspections of Insider Threat Programs

Defense contractors have innumerable responsibilities as listed above that are in addition to the products and services they are paid to provide. Contractors are also required to demonstrate compliance with many government customers and prime contractor requirements. Contractors should protect all classified information that they are provided access to or that they possess. Below we can see where the Insider Threat Program fits; right in the center of mandatory NISPOM requirements:

- Protect classified and controlled unclassified information in their custody
- Appoint Contractor Security Officials
- Appoint Key Management Personnel
- Establish Insider Threat Program
- Develop Standard Practice Procedures
- Cooperate with Federal Agencies
- Provide Security Training and Briefings
- Conduct Security Reviews

ITPSO and FSO

The ITPSO is the focal point for the ITP. They report to the Senior Management Official, just as the Facility Security Officer (FSO) does. The FSO and ITPSO can be the same person. Additionally, the ITPSO / FSO can be an additional delegated task and not necessarily a primary function depending on size of the organization. For example, the ITPSO can also be FSO and senior engineer in a small company. In larger companies, these can be full time positions.

So, the defense contractor task is to integrate an insider threat program under the purview of the government. The first step is to designate the ITPSO (Appendix A) to establish and execute the insider threat program. The ITPSO must be:

- U.S. citizen
- Employee of the organization
- Senior official within the organization
- Security Clearance at the same level as the facility clearance
- If FSO is not the designated official, ensures the FSO is a primary ITP member
- The ITPSO will complete required training
- For multiple facility organizations, contractors may choose to establish an entity wide ITP with one senior official appointed
- Each cleared entity using the entity-wide ITPSO must separately appoint that person as its ITPSO for that facility

The ITPSO must be eligible for a security clearance at the same level as that of the organization's facility clearance level. This requires them to be a U.S. citizen. The senior official designation means that they should be trusted to make decisions beneficial of the organization, be capable of facilitating ITP group meetings, make recommendations, oversee and report results for the entity's senior official to understand and take action.

Also, the ITPSO should be an employee of the company since organizational responsibilities and accountability tasks should never be delegated to external entities. However, while the ITPSO is an organization employee, it may be prudent to outsource tasks and subject matter expertise to consultants or other experts in the field.

The ITPSO executes and establishes the ITP and exercises or facilitates working groups to accomplish the ITP goals. The ITPSO leads through the ITP Working Group (IPTWG) and tackles the insider threat issues, conducts risk assessments, offers solutions, address incidents and prepares reports. The ITPSO should use the working group to execute and oversee the program requirements.

Insider threat programs should have Senior Official buy-in and involvement.

Responsibilities include:

• Manage the program
• Provide resource recommendations
• Submit the implementation plan and annual report
• Ensure proper handling and use of records
• Consult with legal counsel
• Establish guidelines for record retention
• Facilitate oversight reviews to ensure policy compliance

THE INSIDER THREAT PROGRAM WORKING GROUP (ITPWG)

I recommend tackling the ITP with a working group approach. Charter the ITPWG (see Appendix B) and document the ITPWG existence and triggers for establishing an ITPWG session. These meetings should include regular intervals as well as event driven.

The idea is to provide a well-prepared risk management group to protect classified information from unauthorized disclosure. Focus should be set specifically to prevent those without the proper security clearance and need to know from accessing it, as well as protect classified information from malicious activities of a trusted insider with access and need to know. To do so, the ITPWG should place emphasis on:

- Preparing, maintaining, and updating the ITP risk management elements in accordance with ITP requirements and schedules
- Continuously evaluating the application of countermeasures and their effectiveness
- Documenting results and ITP efforts for DCSA or other review
- Briefing ITP status to senior officials and stakeholders

The ITPSO and corporate senior official should guide and train the ITPWGs on the expectations, focus, results, and after-action due outs. The ITPWG should be coordinated and conducted in a location approved for classified or other sensitive level information and classified documentation when required. Though it's not necessary that all ITPWG members have a clearance, discussions and analysis conducted should consider the access and need to know of the members present. It may be necessary to have separate working groups to address unique need to know or sensitivity issues. The members should be aware of NISPOM other national, local or group requirements and address any gaps in ITP application and external requirements.

Gather Data

While the NISPOM applies to CDCs, the following are requirements for government agencies standing up an ITP. Use these to determine what the ITPWG will use as a baseline to gather relevant ITP data. It may be possible that the CDC ITP coordinates with ITPs of government or other contractor locations where the CDCs cleared employees may perform on classified contracts. Developing a symbiotic relationship with other ITPs may be necessary where employees work at other locations. Information sharing resources should be explored.

Otherwise, other references and resources include organic or external capabilities:

- Counterintelligence - this is primarily a government agency capability. However, if information is extended to the CDC, the ITPSO should incorporate the information into the ITP.
- Facility Security Officer or Corporate Security – Include NISPOM reportable topics that the FSO is already covering. Leverage this information for ITPWG analysis. Also include other security issues such as security incidents, parking issues, or other non-NISPOM security events.
- Human resources – Human resources is closely connected to employee issues good or bad. Include any disciplinary actions, terminations, demotions, personnel or interpersonal relationship issues, payroll and voucher files, outside work/activities requests.
- Law enforcement – The ITP may become aware of employee activities from law enforcement blotter reports, court issues, or other behavior triggering reportable events.
- User activity monitoring – User activity monitoring includes access records from badging, video recording, computer access monitoring (printing, uploads, downloads, etc.). This could trigger reportable events such as accessing classified information after hours, transmitting classified information over unclassified means and should be added to the risk assessment.

ITP Procedures

The ITP should include actions for reportable information. Actions could include, discussion, analysis, reporting and response. Such actions should address:

- Threat matter clarification - reportable information could constitute a threat. Evaluate the information provided from the sources and references mentioned above and determine what actions to take.
- Central management of response actions – Once information

is processed, it's time to quantify a potential risk. With the risk analysis comes the requirement to respond with reporting and assigning of mitigations. The ITP should include documenting actions of the ITPWG. This documentation includes:

- Reported threats and response actions
- Timely resolution of matters

Again, even if your facility is not possessing, these tasks are required. Though there may not be a recognizable threat, or classified data, there may be risk where the cleared employees perform classified information off-site, or during classified meetings on-site.

For example, consider that a CDC is non-possessing. Their DD Form 254 indicates that the classified work will be performed at a government or other contractor facility. The ITP can be established to coordinate with the ITPs of the customer or other location where classified information is processed.

Further, consider that the non-possessing CDC learns that there is reportable information about a cleared employee, they will address that with the organic CDC ITP as well as the ITP of the organization where the cleared employee is engaged in classified processing.

The ITPWG at its basic level works with insider SMEs to evaluate information for sensitivity designation. The following functions are within an ITPWG scope:

- Review of security classification guides for evaluating raw data or derivative classification decisions
- Review of DD Forms 254 for instructions on how to protect classified information in the execution of classified contracts
- Review of contract statements of work for performance of work requirements and designation of classified information in raw data or derivative performance
- Designate information processed on classified information systems (computers, networks hard drives)

The ITPWG should also provide oversight and inspection tasks to ensure continuity and consistency of the program. They should also provide tailored guidance during the application of ITP requirements. These requirements and designations should be formally established and documented in writing:

- Implementation of an Insider Threat Program (ITP) to deter and detect suspicious activities or threats (the charter memo in Appendix B serves as documentation)
- Designate a ITP Senior Official (ITPSO) (see Appendix A)
- Train the designated ITPSO, ITP group members and all cleared employees (Appendix D. Use training certificates or sign in sheet to document training)
- Implement classified networks monitoring (if they exist)
- Maintain ITP records (meeting notes and self-inspections)
- Conduct self-inspections of Insider Threat Programs (self-inspection results)

Assemble the ITPWG

Cleared defense contractors have government customers who identify classified information and provide guidance through NISPOM and contracts. In this case, the ITPWG can implement the ITP based on the provided guidance. However, there may be cases where additional sensitive item identification may need to be made where guidance is lacking.

In some cases, the organizations or the customers may not have provided such information or guidance. In these situations, the ITPWG may have to form to evaluate organization products and services to set a protection baseline. This may be more frequent in smaller organizations or boutique businesses creating unique products and services.

Here, the ITPWG will rely on subject matter experts, written policies and procedures, plans, schematics, programmatic documents, etc. to gain a better understanding of what needs to be identified and protected. This understanding is normally gained after reviewing relevant documents available.

The group members should include as a minimum:

- ITPSO
- FSO
- Any capability developers and managers
  - Engineers
  - Program managers
  - Research and development
- Security
- Legal
- Human resources
- Cybersecurity
- IT
- Information System Security Manager (ISSM) / Information System Security Officer (ISSO)
- Subject matter experts from each business unit
- Industry partners or stakeholders
- Where possible or practical it may include members of outside organizations such as:
  - FBI
  - Professional organizations
  - Counterintelligence

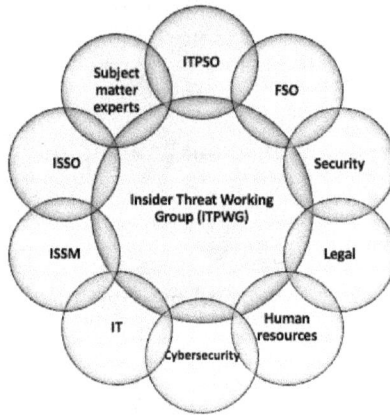

Figure 1 Insider Threat Program Working Group Members

Set the Focus for Non-Possessing CDC ITPWGs

The IPT focus is on protecting classified information, even if not at the CDC facility. The ITPWG should consider the risk to classified information at off-site location and may include coordinating actions with any off-site ITPWGs. Even though a cleared employee may perform classified work at another location, the parent facility ITP efforts can contribute to protecting classified information. The PPWG should focus ITP efforts on any information reported on the cleared employee and coordinate that information with the ITP at the performing organization.

For example, the owning organization is still responsible for providing training to the cleared employee, even if they work at a customer site. They also maintain personnel files, the security clearance, visit requests and security clearance oversight. Additionally, the cleared employees on-site may also be exposed to classified information through meetings and visits.

It may be possible for a cleared employee with little access to classified information to be an insider threat to classified information. The ITPWG should consider the possibilities and be prepared to address them.

Set the Focus For Possessing CDC ITPWGs

In addition to monitoring employees and the actions taken for Non-Possessing ITPs consider protecting the classified information on-site. The ITP focus should be on filtering and prioritizing organization items and information to be protected from insider threat access. It is good to set the focus on the agreed upon criteria.

Keep in mind that even though the customer may provide information marked as classified, your organization may spin off, generate or derive products that require the same level of protection. Each organization is unique and requires ITPWG due diligence to discover and document:

- Raw data
- Generated products
- Unique services and processes
- Test information
- Research results
- Consumer data
- Machine tooling and calibration
- Drawings

The ITPWG should be diverse enough for the leader to facilitate conversation necessary to identify potential insider threat to classified information. The group should identify and document where information resides at the organization and how it is present. For example, the information may be an item, software, document, or softcopy. The key is to identify the existence, the sensitivity level, and where located. See Appendix C for an example. Also consider a third party vendor for a classified information inventory management system.
This task will prove easier when customers identify their information

to be protected. For example, if classified information is provided for work on a defense contract, the information or items will be marked with a classification level. It will require storage and performance per the NISPOM. If the FSO is not the ITPSO, they will at least serve on the ITPWG and be instrumental to ensure classified information is accounted for. The FSO can present compliance with NISPOM requirements to the IPTWG. The ITPSO can ensure the FSO's efforts are included in the ITP risk assessment.

The more difficult task is identifying sensitive information that is generated on-site and derived from customer provided classified information that is marked or already documented. This requires the ITPWG to assess the organization's mission, business units, and capability developers to identify sensitive information.

ITPWG Steps

The following steps may be adapted as ITPWG agenda topics and implemented to assist with the ITPWG focus. Using the topics, the ITPWG can develop an actionable plan to execute the ITP and measure compliance and effectiveness, as well as answer the self-inspection questions identified earlier. The next few sections will focus on the five steps. ITPWGs might add to the steps as necessary based on experience, organization processes, or other factors.

1. Gather reportable information
Identify / Document Existence and Location of Classified Information
2. Determine / Document Vulnerabilities
   - Determine / Document Protection Requirements
   - Assume a Threat
3. Assess Current Protection Measures
4. Assign Additional Protection
5. Establish Insider Threat Reporting Procedures and Response Plans
6. Train the Force

The ITPWG should be strictly focused on insider threat and protection issues. Avoid the temptation to discuss other issues that are not insider threat based or are not on the approved agenda. For example, the ITPWG may form to discuss the protection of classified items as they go to a test event. The discussion should focus on preventing insiders from committing espionage or accessing classified information for nefarious purposes. The discussion should address the classified information during preparation, transportation, storage, test result generation and messaging. The results should ensure consistent protection according to marking and distribution requirements, OPSEC considerations, and countermeasures. Any discussion outside of the scope should be avoided.

Documenting ITP Application

I had a boss that used to say, "never let them see you sweat." There is wisdom in this statement when it comes to instilling confidence with inspectors. Auditors and inspectors use a checklist and have an agenda. Their task is to ensure the answers are satisfactory and the inspection subjects are applying processes appropriately. What they don't have time for is someone who has no way to answer questions in an intelligent manner. They also don't have time to interpret confusing answers, even if the subject is compliant with requirements, it's not up to the investigator to pull the answers out.

The ITPWG ensures that the ITPSO is well prepared to both confidently answer questions and have the tools on hand to demonstrate sound application of processes. To do so, the plan should include written documentation of every required element. This documentation should be maintained and readily available for internal and external review. As a review, documentation should include the following (Use appendices for sample documentation artifacts):

- The existence of the ITP.
- The appointment of the ITPSO and FSO
- The establishment of the ITPWG

- Methodology to gather reportable information
- A reporting process
- An incident response process
- The existence of protected items and information by name, format and location (ITP Asset inventory)
- Current Protection
- Recommended Additional Protection
- Training Execution

The ITPWG should assign a note taker to capture important comments, decisions, agenda items, assignments and accountability of tasks. The notes serve as a vehicle for moving forward and capturing decisions for historical value. The ITPWG decisions may successfully move forward with the ITP or they could eventually be removed as contracts expire or revisited as contracts are won. As the ITPWG decisions move forward, are cancelled or are resurrected with new contract requirements, the historical notes will play a valuable role in consistency and rationale for decision making. The ITPSO should also understand what to do with meeting notes, actions taken and assigned, holding members accountable for actions and timelines, and how to share information with leaders and comply with laws.

The ITPWG meeting agendas should include the review of available security classification guides, DD 254s, statements of work, and other relevant documentation relating to classified information protection requirements. The ITPWG should assess additional necessary protection and address with enforced need to know and accountability measures. This ensures consistency of protection.

CHAPTER 6 POSSESSING FACILITIES

This chapter is for CDCs with classified information processed and stored on -ite. The first few sections include NISPOM best practices as well as enhanced Need to Know (NTK) procedures to address many insider threat issues. In the next section of this chapter, we will cover monitoring for processing classified information on information systems.

Capture the existence of classified information by location and how it manifests. For example, you might have classified documents stored in a security container or software in a classified lab. It is important for the ITPWG to incorporate reportable information on cleared employees with the understanding where the information is, how it manifests and how it is protected. This combined information should be assessed, risk quantified, and any actionable events reported and responded to.

IDENTIFY / DOCUMENT EXISTENCE AND LOCATION OF SENSITIVE INFORMATION

One way to successfully implement an ITP is to understand what needs to be protected. One might be tempted to say everything is critical and lock down the organization. Using this scenario, you can ensure 100% protection, but at the cost of doing 0% business. Everything can be stolen or sabotaged, but not everything will have the same impact. Focusing on the most valuable and vulnerable items or information is critical to the ITP success. In addition to reporting guidance required of all CDCs, possessing CDCs should include asset protection. The ITPWG adds the following to the charter and agenda:

- Identifying classified information under the organization's control

- Identifying vulnerabilities to classified information
- Identifying and implementing information, system, cyber, physical security and appropriate disciplines to mitigate vulnerabilities.
- Developing tailored guidance that employees can use to implement the countermeasures

Value

This methodology for risk reduction begins with documenting what items or information will make the most impact if exploited and understanding what that impact will be. Thinly spreading focus to all assets would exhaust valuable resources and increase danger to the most vulnerable assets. The ITP focus should be narrowed in scope to the oversight requirements. For cleared DoD contractors, the focus is on U.S. Government classified information as identified in 32 CFR Part 117 (NISPOM). Others without classified information might create a similar scope.

This focus does not mean other information is not important, but is filtered and prioritized. In many cases, while the ITP focuses on mission essential or other sensitive information, personnel security and safety, financial status, quality assurance and other topics are covered by other disciplines within the organization. For example, employees are the most important asset to any organization. While the ITP may not be focused on employee safety, the organization understands that there are safety and security disciplines and requirements already at work. Additionally, phone numbers and points of contact are worth protecting from the general public, however, there are other forces at work that already protect that information and segregate it from normal communication channels.

The ITP simply focuses on enhancing and elevating the priority of classified information and items that could cause some level of damage to the U.S. if a trusted employee exploited it. The most valuable and vulnerable items and information should have a robust and layered protection effort. This leaves classified information protected while in use, in storage, in transport, and in all states of existence. This protection should include how to prevent unauthorized access through mitigations that deter and detect.

DETERRENCE AND DETECTION

Deterrence and detection is key to an ITP's success. Where in traditional security, deterrence and detection may be used to protect items and information from unauthorized access, the ITP may want to trace and account for access by authorized personnel as well. Think of authorized persons at this point as having access, but need to know is not yet determined. Deterrence that prevents access and detection that reports actions of authorized and unauthorized persons may prove to lead to a successful ITP. This proactive method allows the identification and location of protected information and items as well as keeping up with the activity status of items and those who access. This type of protective action allows the ITP to better demonstrate a program of positive control.

Protection begins with documenting classified information as it manifests and controlling access to it. The ITP's role is to recognize the existence, assess risk, and train the workforce. Prior to documenting the risk and applying countermeasures, the ITPWG should work within the organization and subject matter experts to identify exactly what needs to be protected and how it manifests in the organization.

In other words, it's OK to understand that there may be a desire for threat actors to access sensitive information. The first step is for the ITPWG to consider what the insider might desire to obtain and the value of it or impact. The ITPWG should ensure the organization is engaged to identify, mark and protect specific sensitive information.

In many cases, insider threat risk reduction doesn't require exhaustive efforts by the ITPWG. The ITPWG can leverage existing corporate policy, procedures and risk reduction efforts without having to create additional processes and procedures. For example, the FSO has already established security programs to protect classified information, export compliance employees may have identified export controlled items and HR may have HIPPA efforts documented. In these cases, the ITPWG gathers the information and documents how ITP is engaged.

GOVERNMENT OR CUSTOMER INFORMATION

The first place to start is with information that is already identified as protected. This includes classified information, controlled unclassified information, and export controlled information. Outside of the cleared defense contractor requirements, you may include the customer information they have identified as protected. This information is provided by a government or prime contractor customer or the defense contractors. This could be personal, financial or other information that is generally sensitive. It's up to the group to define the priority.

If the customer has already provided guidance on protecting their information, then the ITPWG should document these requirements and incorporate into the ITP.

TYPES OF CUSTOMER INFORMATION

Government Agency Classified Information

If you are a cleared defense contractor with classified information in inventory, then you already understand that security classification guidance, classification markings, and DD Forms 254 are on hand that already requires marking and protecting classified information. For Department Of Defense (DoD) information, guidance is found in NISPOM as discussed earlier.

Government Agency Controlled Unclassified Information

Government customers may have already identified information provided as Controlled Unclassified Information (CUI). If so, this information should be protected from unauthorized access per the

DoD CUI program guidelines. This guidance should be incorporated into the ITP tasks.

The FSO, program managers, contracts managers and key employees should understand where to find classified, export controlled and CUI information. The FSO has the best understanding of where classified information exists and how it resides on site.

However, other sources include the DD Form 254, Statement of Work or other contractual guidance. The DD Form 254 describes the classified work to be conducted and the statement of work includes other additional work performance objectives (other than classified). All are very important in determining what the customer is providing as well as any additional classified, export controlled, CUI or other sensitive information that may be generated or derived as products are developed.

Generated Information

In the course of conducting research and development the organization may generate additional products that share characteristics of information that may already be classified. However, since it is not owned by or directed by the U.S. Government, it may not be classified, but should be treated as classified. The ITPWG should ensure that protection measures such as identification, marking and processing are accomplished for any work generated.

Derived Information

While working with customer information the organization may generate additional products that require the same amount of protection as the originally documented information. The ITPWG should ensure that protection measures such as identification, marking and processing are accomplished for any work generated.

Once the ITPWG has a good understanding of derived classified information, they should identify how to identify and mark this information that may be produced as raw data. This could be new end items, printed documents, computer documents, software or other items. The task is to help SMEs working with the information determine how to mark and protect it and the IPTWG oversee the application.

Once classified information is identified and marked they are now priority items to protect from insider threat actors.

The government or prime contractor describes and funds the classified contracts, but the cleared defense contractor designs and builds. The ITPWG should consider the following while evaluating the ITP and information:

- Who is responsible for generating sensitive data?
- Who is held responsible for security, export controlled, or policy violations?

The ITPWG should consult with organization subject matter experts to include any recommendations from existing contracts and customer engagement to determine which, if any, requirements are applicable to current contracts. Then they should analyze the results.

Sensitive Item Name / PM or Project Lead	How sensitive item manifests (End item, Hardcopy, Softcopy, Software)	How sensitive item is / to be marked (Classified, CUI, Export Controlled Organizational Markings)
Program XYZ Performance Parameters / Jay Betho	Hardcopy	SECRET

Table 1 Document Existing Sensitive Information

NISPOM and best practices recommend that classified information be part of an Information Management System (IMS) or inventory management. Where FSOs are accounting for the existence of classified information, this should be leveraged and documented in the ITP. This is a good practice since DCSA may want to investigate accountability processes. Where an IMS exists for classified information, Table 1 may not be necessary and the IMS can be leveraged for ITP purposes. I also recommend that other organizations enter their sensitive information and leverage in their ITPs in a similar manner.

If no IMS exists, use Table 1 to document. Use the three categories as they can be tailored for the sensitive information specific to the organization. This accountability will be necessary for assessing risk and assigning protective measures.

In the first column, list the name of the sensitive item and the name of contract PM or Project Lead. It could be a specific name of an item, a title of a paper, software, or description of a process. This should be specific to the item so there is no mistake of what the item is. However, we recommend that the name itself not be sensitive or the list itself will need protection. The named lead(s) are responsible for identifying need to know or designating need to know tasks

In the How Sensitive Item Manifests, document the format. I recommended a few options (End item, Hardcopy, Softcopy, Software), but feel free to modify. It's important to describe the format as each may require different protection.

In the final column, list the markings to be applied. For example, for classified you might list Confidential, Secret, or Top Secret. You might list CUI or Export Controlled if tracking in your ITP.

CHAPTER 7 VULNERABILITIES

Since we are not addressing a particular threat by name, we will use a process to focus on vulnerabilities to classified information. One method is to conduct the following:

- Identify Required Protection Measures
- Assume a Threat Exists

IDENTIFY REQUIRED PROTECTION MEASURES

NISPOM Requirements

For NISPOM, this doesn't need to be documented in the ITP as it is under the FSO tasks. Again, the FSO's efforts should be leveraged and documented for ITP purposes. This section is for mandated countermeasures such as are required by federal government and customer directives. For the purpose of this book, we will focus on the 32 CFR Part 117 (NISPOM), The International Traffic In Arms Regulation (ITAR), and Controlled Unclassified Information. In your situation there may be more, or fewer, requirements. The ITPWG should determine which apply and tailor to the organization.

The NISPOM addresses the U.S. government classified information that are in the cleared defense contractor's possession. The requirements are implemented by the Facility Security Office and their team. Since the FSO is either part of the ITP or serves as the ITPSO, they have already documented the existence of the classified information or items, how they are protected and where they reside. At its very basic level, classified information should be protected as follows:

- Access is provided with security clearance and need to know

- TOP SECRET - In a secure container (safe or vault) with monitored intrusion detection systems
- SECRET and CONFIDENTIAL - In a secure container (safe or vault)

NISPOM requires that before an employee can access classified information, they should have a security clearance and Need to Know (NTK). Security clearance is awarded based on an investigation and adjudication processes. Once a clearance is granted, the FSO authorizes access in the national database, the employee is notified and they are authorized to access classified information if they have NTK.

The NISPOM explains the protection requirements for classified information by classification level. Generally, NISPOM requires a GSA Security Container to store SECRET and below classified information. In certain situations the same information can be stored in an approved classified area with an alarm system. Again, see the FSO, NISPOM and other references at the end of the book for specific details for protecting classified information. This book is focused on the insider threat to classified information protected according to NISPOM.

To address the insider threat issue, consider that NISPOM based best practices for accessing classified at a CDC location including both centralized and decentralized holdings. Both centralized and decentralized holdings should be taken into account and risk equation as the ITPWG conducts its business.

Centralized holdings occur where all classified information is under the control of a document control position for items or softcopy and hardcopy documents. For information systems, this is usually in the form of hard drives, other computer media or classified networks.

Decentralized holdings refer to situations where classified information is dispersed throughout the CDC and under the control of individuals with approved storage at their locations.

For Non-NISPOM ITP Inclusion

Cleared Defense Contractors are not yet required to include CUI
as part of the DCSA reviews or the ISP. However, you may consider
adding to the ITP scope if time and resources permit. I anticipate this
will be a requirement in the future. Refer to our book, *Establishing a
CUI Program* for more information on CUI programs. Leverage the
program recommendations for the ITP. The information in this section
is a recommendation of how to, proceed if the ITP should include CUI.
Otherwise, you can focus on classified information and move to the
next section.

The ITAR focuses on dual use technologies and items that are export
controlled. This is based on the United States Munitions List (USML)
which identifies critical technologies that must be prevented from
export without permission (licenses and proviso) from the U.S.
government. This oversight usually falls under an export control senior
official, FSO or other responsible person in the organization who
should be part of the ITP. At its very basic level, ITAR information
should be protected from access of any non-U.S. person whether at the
facility or internationally. If classified, it should be protected as above
and should be segregated, stored, or protected from non-U.S. persons
who do not have a valid need to know or export license. If unclassified
this ITAR controlled information should be segregated, stored, or
protected from non-U.S. persons who do not have a valid need to know
or export license.

CUI is government information that has been identified as to be
excluded from public release. It should be protected from access by
anyone without an official government contract or other need to know
determination. CUI could also be ITAR controlled. CUI should be
protected similar to ITAR controlled above and should be segregated,
stored, or protected from non-U.S. persons or anyone else who does
not have a valid need to know or export license.

For example, mandated countermeasures for CUI and ITAR controlled information includes:

During Working Hours

• Personnel must take care not to expose CUI to unauthorized users or others who do not have a lawful government purpose to see the information.

• CUI cover sheets (not required) may be placed on top of documents to conceal the contents from casual viewing.

• Always control or protect CUI with at least one physical barrier and take reasonable care to ensure that the information is protected from unauthorized access and observation.

After Working Hours

• Store in unlocked containers, desks, or cabinets only if facility provides continuous monitoring. If not, CUI must be in a locked desk, file cabinet, locked room or where security measures are in place to prevent or detect unauthorized access.

• Locked container should indicate it contains CUI.

• Do Not store CUI in public areas (car, home office, etc.) or view while on public transportation.

The following should be documented as in Table 2.

Sensitive Item Name / PM or Project Lead	How sensitive item manifests (End item, Hardcopy, Softcopy, Software)	How sensitive item is marked (Classified, CUI, Export Controlled Organizational Markings)	Mandated Protection
Program XYZ Performance Parameters / Jay Betho	Hardcopy	SECRET	GSA Approved Security Container

Table 2 Mandated Protection

The first three columns identify what requires protection, how it exists and how it is marked. The next column should be used to describe protective measures that are required by local policy, contract, NISPOM. This column should list protection by item and format. The final column should list the source of the mandate.

Assume a Threat Exists

Adversaries target desired technology and focus on stealing or sabotaging it. The rational is they don't have to expend research and development resources. It's much cheaper to target a capability and determine methods to acquire it. The impact to the victim is loss in capability, technology or effectiveness.

Consider that research and development is an expensive endeavor. It is much cheaper to acquire technology through reverse engineering, requests for information or theft. While it is illegal to provide any export to some countries; adversaries may try to circumvent laws with implementing creative methods of obtaining what they need.

A good practice is to develop a process to allow access to only those with security clearance and need to know. The rationale is that not every employee needs to know intimate details about every effort. Once the ITPWG helps identify protected information, they can also oversee those activities and assist with determining who should be provided access, limit access, and account for the sensitive information. There are many methods an adversary can use to exploit vulnerabilities while targeting employees. These methodologies focus on their understanding of what is important and the impact to their efforts. For example, if an organization is known for building combat vehicles, then the adversary searching for that information may begin efforts to recruit an engineer who designs tanks and has access to valuable information.

It would be prudent for the ITPWG to identify where this information resides and begin investigating how an employee might exfiltrate it or how an adversary might access it. Some questions might be:

• Who is authorized access to sensitive information (based on clearance level and need to know)?
• How is limited access enforced if at all (prevent unauthorized personnel from gaining access)?

The answers to the above questions can identify some vulnerabilities. The IPTWG should answer these questions as they pertain to prioritized sensitive information. Again, bringing in the FSO or other security professional can ensure classified information and other high priority information is covered as required in NISPOM and other regulatory guidance.

More proactive measures include theft or interception through hacking or posing as authorized recipient. Refer to Table 3 to document vulnerabilities.

Sensitive Item Name / PM or Project Lead	How sensitive item manifests (End item, Hardcopy, Softcopy, Software)	How sensitive item is marked (Classified, CUI, Export Controlled Organizational Markings)	Mandated Protection	Insider Threat Vulnerabilities
Program XYZ Performance Parameters / Jay Betho	Hardcopy	SECRET	GSA Approved Security Container	Security container is in common areas. Security container holds classified information from multiple contracts

Table 3 Vulnerabilities

The first three columns identify what needs protection, how it exists, how it is marked and how it should be protected. The next column should be used to describe how the information is vulnerable or how it can be exploited. This vulnerability equals the ability for an insider to exploit the information. In this case, classified information is consolidated and anyone with a clearance can access it. This leaves classified information vulnerable as there are no need to know countermeasures.

CHAPTER 8 ASSESS PROTECTION MEASURES

Using this approach, the IPTWG should have a good understanding of what to protect, where it exists by name and location, mandatory or regulated countermeasures and how a threat may manifest itself, it's time to assess how well that protection is in place. Current protections may be adequate for a successful NISPOM application, however, understanding and applying insider specific vulnerabilities may point to gaps in protection. The important task now is to document that the ITP is up to date.

Documenting current countermeasures is a valuable practice and has many applications. Those readers who have not been under review may make the mistake of assuming audit or reviews are conducted with yes or no types of questions such as: "Do you have a program in place?", "Have you appointed a responsible person?", "Do you provide receipts for transactions of classified information?". However, more seasoned professionals understand that the reviews are demonstration driven or essay types of questions. These questions are similar to those posed earlier in this book. Documenting your ITP the way this book recommends may result in more positive experiences with the auditor or reviewer.

Use questions as posed earlier as well as in the *Self-Inspection Handbook for NISP Contractors*. These questions and inspection points force the action of identifying where classified information exists and the protective measures that should be in place. By using the self-inspection criteria, the ITPWG can see in real time what is being accomplished. Of course, the FSO is already doing this and if so, the act of conducting the self-inspection, findings, and gaps can be annotated for the ITP purposes.

It is not necessary to list each and every countermeasure at this point as it is already captured by the FSO. The ITP simply can document that the inspections are ongoing, the dates conducted and that the results are recorded with the FSO.

Sensitive Item Name / PM or Project Lead	How sensitive item manifests (End item, Hardcopy, Softcopy, Software)	How sensitive item is marked (Classified, CUI, Export Controlled Organizational Markings)	Mandated Protection	Insider Threat Vulnerabilities	Assessment
Program XYZ Performance Parameters / Jay Betho	Hardcopy	SECRET	GSA Approved Security Container	Security container is in common areas. Security container holds classified information from multiple contracts	Meets NISPOM requirements. However, must have need to know enforcement measures. At this point, any cleared employee can access classified information for multiple contracts

Table 4 Define Gaps in Protection

While this paragraph may be the shortest, it may be the most important to the developing ITPWG. The impact is that while the NISPOM may provide adequate countermeasures, it may not be enough to stop the insider threat. Looking at protecting classified information through the lens of an adversary recruiting a trusted insider, the ITPWG can recognize a glaring vulnerability; unhindered access.

When the cleared employee is initially an authorized employee solely based on security clearance level, it is difficult to determine an insider threat action. For example, in Tables 2 and 3, classified information is protected against unauthorized intruders or unauthorized employees (without security clearances) from accessing SECRET information. Multiple layers of security might exist including guards, gates, alarms and security containers. The organization can keep non-employees and uncleared employees away pretty easily. The idea is that it takes extra effort and tools to access the classified information.

However, Table 4 tells a different story. In Table 4, the ITPWG realized that everyone with a SECRET clearance is authorized access to any classified information. In our example consider that the security container contains classified information from multiple contracts. Each contract has different engineers with different work projects. Project 1 provides products for a missile system and Project 2 works on RADARS for a different customer.

Countermeasures in place protect classified information from unauthorized access by outsiders. However, it doesn't protect access to Project 1 information from employees working on Project 2, which would be a security violation. The ITPWG realizes that additional countermeasures are needed to enforce need to know. Once in place, not everyone with a clearance will be authorized, only those with clearance and need to know.

Everyone with a SECRET clearance should not be authorized to access any classified information. Many understand the concept, but it's difficult to apply. Realizing that any employee can acquire any classified information based solely on security clearance can lead to a realization that there is a glaring hole in protection. Enforcing need to know can further refine what authorized and unauthorized access looks like. Adding an extra layer of protection by enforcing need to know suddenly creates an opportunity to further define authorized access.

CHAPTER 9 ASSIGN ADDITIONAL PROTECTION

Where security clearances are easier to determine, Need To Know (NTK) is more difficult to enforce. The holder of the classified information can determine from the top level down (national data base) that someone has a security clearance, but it may be more difficult to determine need to know. This is usually established from the bottom level up, meaning it's based on direct contribution to a project or work effort.

Getting back to NISPOM best practices, we can build onto the best practices to ensure NTK is enforced to protect classified information from the authorized insider threat. The ITPWG should consider protection above NISPOM guidance to protect classified information from the insider threat. Current NISPOM guidelines for using security containers to store classified information, setting alarms, and using access management protects classified information from unauthorized persons. These common safeguards used to protect classified information from unauthorized access, don't always protect from classified information from those with security clearances but without need to know.

Need to Know requires an additional layer of protection

Many people focus on the number of cleared employees as too many and seek ways to reduce that number. However, the emphasis should not be limiting the number of cleared employees, but limiting what they can access. Need to know enforcement provides insider threat red flags. A look back at the case studies demonstrates that those with clearances and without need to know raised suspicion when attempting to access classified information they were cleared for, but without the need to know.

Recall from the earlier presented use cases that classified information was requested from people with clearances but did not work on the project. For example, in the case of Ron Rockwell Hansen, the enforced NTK worked. Hansen had to recruit another insider to get the documents his hander requested. This led to the reporting that led to his capture.

However, if a Cleared Defense Contractor (CDC) does not enforce NTK, anyone could access the classified information. For example, in the case of Regan, he had unmitigated access to a classified network to access information he did not typically work with. Also, consider an example of decentralized classified document storage. A CDC stores all the SECRET documents in a GSA approved security container and all the people that have access to the container have SECRET clearances. Technically, this meets NISPOM requirements. However, NTK is violated if all the employees work on different projects.

If an employee works on propulsion has access to documents for a high energy laser project, they could be able to get unfettered access for a handler outside of their normal work efforts. If they were to be recruited, and they did not trip any reporting alarms, NTK would be a last effort. Without NTK, the person could access this information continuously. Need to know can be enforced in many ways, here are a few examples:

- Material contribution - this is based on work performance. Where material contribution is basis for NTK countermeasures can be applied specific to the work performance. For example, if an employee accepts a new position, they should be removed from access instead of allowing access for the traditional two week notice.
- Contract number - This is broader and less specific, but it is a means to enforce need to know. It allows for insider threat countermeasures similar to material contribution.
- Working group - This is very specific. For example, cleared employees involved in a ITPWG will have access to ITPWG decisions. Cleared employees outside of the group will be outside of the access.

Working group employees can limit access based on the relationship After identifying what is sensitive, the ITPWG should review where sensitive information manifests and apply additional and appropriate countermeasures focused on published ITP requirements and internal goals. For example, minimum guidance exists in NISPOM, ITAR and other regulatory documents, but may not be strong enough to protect against trusted employees.

Classified Information has proscribed countermeasures found in the National Industrial Security Program Manual (NISPOM). Classified information should be marked appropriately as CONFIDENTIAL, SECRET, and TOP SECRET. CONFIDENTIAL and SECRET information should be stored at a minimum in a GSA approved container or vault. TOP SECRET information requires supplemental controls such as an intrusion detection system.

Leverage the FSO and NISPOM

The FSO may also serve as the ITPSO. If this is not the case, the FSO should be a vital member of the ITP. The ITP should apply classified information to the risk assessment in coordination with the FSO and ITP required member. The FSO runs the security program designed to protect classified information and should provide adequate input to the ITP. ITP oversight and actions should work under the scope of NISPOM and will not be covered here. If you desire more information on protecting classified information, please consult the FSO, NISPOM, and resources found at the end of this book.

It would be prudent for the ITPWG to identify where this information resides and begin investigating how an employee might exfiltrate it or how an adversary might access it. As listed earlier, these questions might be:

• Where is this information located (in a safe, in a computer, on a drawing, in a garage, on a network)?
• How does it exist (hardcopy, software, softcopy, end item, thumb

drive, removable media, etc)?
- Who is authorized access to sensitive information (based on clearance level and need to know)?
- How is limited access enforced if at all (prevent unauthorized personnel from gaining access)?
- Who is required to have access with clearance and need to know?
- Who actually has access that may not have clearance and need to know?
- Is there a need to know roster?
- What type of insiders have access to areas but not the sensitive information?
    o Consultant
    o Partner
    o Vendor
    o Repair persons
    o Employee
    o Support staff
- Where is sensitive information stored?
- Where is sensitive information worked?
- Where is testing conducted?

The answers to the above questions can identify some additional vulnerabilities to be addressed. The IPTWG should answer these questions as they pertain to prioritized sensitive information. Again, bringing in the FSO or other security professional can ensure classified information and other high priority information is covered as required in NISPOM and other regulatory guidance.

Most vulnerabilities can be addressed with enforcing NTK. Material contribution us a factor to justifying need to know. One way to reduce vulnerability to develop the ITP to limit access to include those who have need to know. While NISPOM mentions need to know, most countermeasures required are general in nature and not NTK focused. Your ITP can add the need to know element to the NISPOM countermeasures. Additionally, these need to know recommendations apply to any organization whether defense contractor or public enterprise.

For example, a GSA approved container is required to store classified information. Additionally, restricted areas can be established to perform on classified projects. Once an organization secures classified information according to NISPOM requirements, there is yet another step, determining who gets access. It's not enough to lock information up, the tricky part is determining which employees have a material contribution to the information.

Use Case: An FSO conducted an investigation to determine if classified information was disclosed in an unauthorized manner. The organization was a CDC with more than 20 years of working on classified contracts. In this case, cleared employee #1 asked cleared employee #2 to watch their classified information while they took a break. While on break, employee #2 was summoned to their boss and forgot about the classified information. Employee #1 returned and found the classified information was unattended and reported it to their chain of command. The investigation supported the fact that employee #2 was negligent in leaving the classified information unattended. However, employee #1 was also found negligent in that employee #2 did not have need to know. They should have never been given access to the classified information they were watching. Enforcing need to know would have prevented the security incident.

Determining additional security measures can be applied through NTK determination and enforcement. Need to know should be determined by the holder. However, supervisors and subject matter experts should be involved in the justification of NTK. The following questions are helpful and can be used by the ITPWG if required for the ITP:

- Who is authorized access to which information?
- Who gets access to alarm codes?
- Who gets access to safe combinations?
- Who gets access to restricted areas?

Answering the question, How can access be limited (how do we enforce need to know)? leads to the final question of, How can we implement countermeasures to limit access (establish countermeasures)?

While NISPOM does not require such accountability and enforcement, the following are very effective countermeasures to insider threat issues. See the table below and in Appendix E.

Centralized document control
The person requiring classified information provides a written request that justifies need to know. Once request is made, the document custodian reviews request and any additional NTK guidance before providing requested information.

Inventory management
Enter all classified information into an inventory management system and annotated by classification level, how it manifests, how to determine need to know and current status. Not only can need to know be enforced, but if an item is "checked out" the status will identify who checked it out and will require a checked in action.

Review employee access records
These records include information from inventory management system, badge readers, alarm systems, video monitoring, and even combination lock access logs (built-in benefit of modern combination locks). These records can be reviewed by ITPWG to determine employee activity, alarm and lock successful access and attempts. Anomalies should be reported and addressed.

CLASSIFIED AND UNCLASSIFIED INFORMATION SYSTEMS

Monitoring user activity helps identify users who are abusing their access and may be potential insider threats. The ITPSO should use the ITPWG to decide what to monitor and how to monitor.
As a minimum, CDCs should monitor computer usage. As reviewed in use cases, both unclassified and classified networks can be used to

exploit classified information. Monitoring employee network activity can reveal reportable information for insider threat consideration.

The CDC should establish user monitoring policies and procedures that all employees agree to and sign, understanding that their activity will be monitored. Consider internal monitoring as well as using third party monitoring to capture any insider threat concerns or activities triggered by the system administrator.

The CDCs should establish policies with respect to:

- Personnel usernames and aliases - This allows the CDC to understand who is being monitored as well as direct actions for insider threat activity response.
- Levels of network access - This allows the CDC to enforce need to know as a rationale for access. The system administrator can limit a user's access based on many criteria.
- Unauthorized use of removable media – This should trigger an insider threat response. Employees who bypass policy to upload or download data should at the very least understand that the actions will be investigated.
- Print logs – This is similar to unauthorized upload and download. Print logs provides and additional layer of protection.
- IT audit logs – This allows monitoring of any information system and may lead to discovering suspicious behavior or insider threat activity.

Implementing effective policies and procedures is in itself a countermeasure to detect, report and investigate insider threat activity. Policies protect authorized use, detect unauthorized use and provides analysis of activity on information systems and networks. Table 5 provides an example of applying Insider Threat Countermeasures.

Sensitive Item Name / PM or Project Lead	How sensitive item manifests (End item, Hardcopy, Soft-copy, Software)	How sensitive item is marked (Classified, CUI, Export Controlled Organizational Markings)	Mandated Protection	Insider Threat Vulnerabilities	Insider Threat Countermea-sures
Program XYZ Performance Parameters / Jay Betho	Hardcopy	SECRET	GSA Approved Security Container	Security container is in common areas. Security container holds classified information from multiple contracts.	Limit need to know by one or more of the following to enhance NTK: Centralize container and require employees to "check out" or request documents. Acquire GSA container with separate locking drawers. Acquire additional GSA containers for each contract.

Table 5 Insider Threat Countermeasures

The final column continues our example of moving from everyone with a clearance having authorized access to some are authorized and some are not based on need to know. Where working employees from Project 1 and Project 2 co-mingled their classified information into a security container, the ITPWG realized that they could not enforce need to know. They determined that additional countermeasures as described in this chapter could be applied to limit the amount of authorized users.

They applied a system of centralized access where the security container is under the control of a cleared employee who would provide documents upon request and after reviewing need to know rosters.

Another option is to provide a security container with multiple locking drawers to store each project's work in a separate drawer with a separate combination. Only those with a security clearance and need to know could access the documents.

An additional option would be to buy additional security containers and place classified documents from each project into a separate lockable container.

Once in place, these countermeasures would raise red flags when any employee from project 2 desiring access to Project 1 would be considered an insider threat.

CHAPTER 10 REPORTING

Now that we have established how to protect classified information from an insider threat, providing an actionable response to an insider threat event is critical. Again, we can leverage current NISPOM requirements for an effective response.

The technology and information residing in U.S. cleared defense contractor facilities s is under constant and pervasive threat from foreign intelligence entities seeking to gain the technological edge. Threat activity is a primary reason why reporting is required. CDCs should develop methods for employees to recognize and immediately report suspicious activities, behaviors, and contacts. This book's goal is to create those triggers that indicate an insider threat.

The FSO already provides reporting guidance per NISPOM and Security Executive Agent Directive (SEAD) 3. Under these requirements, cleared individuals should alert the FSO and/or ITPSO to the reportable activities. Reports include information about the individual themselves and other cleared individual activities the individual may become aware of. These should be credible reports and not of rumor or gossip, focusing on potential security or counterintelligence (CI) concerns. Examples of reportable information follow, but keep in mind that this may not be an all-inclusive list on what to report and there may be additional observations not covered.

Leverage FSO Tasks

Our goal is to leverage existing FSO responsibilities as published in NISPOM and the SEADs. That means everything in this book is new content specifically for the ITP. The ITP should leverage what the FSO is already required to do. What this means is that if the existing reporting requirements triggers, the ITP should consider it.

For example, the ITPWG forms to address a reportable incident. In the course of the meeting, the group agrees that classified information access and need to know triggers have not been activated. While the incident is reported, the classified information has been adequately protected. This protection has been confirmed by those who validate the need to know and assessed by the ITP interaction with cleared employees, the supervisors and the FSO. All meetings and interactions have been adequately recorded. In the case of CDCs with no classified information on-site, the reports should be collected and an assessment should be made after coordinating with the ITP of the location possessing classified information.

Continuing the example, the FSO brings up a potential issue for discussion. A few days prior to the meeting, a cleared employee reported credible information that another employee had taken vacation to Europe without reporting it to the FSO. The FSO communicates that this is significant as SEAD 3 requires approval prior to travel. The FSO wants to make the ITPWG aware that an investigation is occurring and that they will report on the progress to keep the ITPWG up to date.

While the incident is being handled through the FSO channels, the ITPWG can consider it as a risk factor. The point is, that the ITPWG may not ever have become aware of the issue and that they should not be running the operation to catch this behavior. However, the system worked, and they should leverage the information. Now they can take a closer look at the classified information that the cleared employee could influence to see if there is an insider threat issue.

Other leveraged adverse information events require greater effort to get cleared employees to understand reporting value. These incidents are usually viewed as an administrative drill such as life changes and include:

- personal status
- name

- marital status (i.e., marriage or divorce)
- citizenship

Adverse information is any information regarding a cleared employee or employee, in process for a clearance or has a clearance, that suggests that his/her ability to safeguard classified information may be impaired or that his or her access to classified information may not be in the interest of national security. Cleared personnel should have a means to report adverse information regarding themselves or another cleared individual.

The following are behaviors that FSOs are required to report. They should trigger reporting and coordination with the ITPWG. Any activity that raises doubts as to whether another covered individual's continued national security eligibility is clearly consistent with the interests of national security. The adverse information reporting identifies 13 topics:

- Adjudicative Guideline A: Allegiance to the United States
- Adjudicative Guideline B: Foreign Influence
- Adjudicative Guideline C: Foreign Preference
- Adjudicative Guideline D: Sexual Behavior
- Adjudicative Guideline E: Personal Conduct
- Adjudicative Guideline F: Financial Considerations - Unexplained affluence or excessive indebtedness.
- Adjudicative Guideline G: Alcohol Consumption - Alcohol abuse
- Adjudicative Guideline H: Drug Involvement - Illegal use or misuse of drugs or drug activity.
- Adjudicative Guideline I: Psychological Conditions - Apparent or suspected mental health issues where there is reason to believe it may impact the covered individual's ability to protect classified information or other information specifically prohibited by law from disclosure
- Adjudicative Guideline J: Criminal Conduct
- Adjudicative Guideline K: Handling Protected Information
- Adjudicative Guideline L: Outside Activities

- Adjudicative Guideline M: Use of Information Technology Systems

Since ITPs are important, why not take time to develop a program to ensure employees continue to demonstrate ethical and legal activity that ensured their employment in the first place? Identify what needs to be protected, enforce clearance and need to know requirements, and foster a healthy reporting environment. If not, an employee could volunteer, be pressured or coerced to steal data or items.

The behaviors that FSOs are required to report should trigger response by and coordination with the ITPWG. Any activity that raises doubts as to whether another covered individual's continued national security eligibility is clearly consistent with the interests of national security.

Adverse information is any information regarding a cleared employee or employee, in process for a clearance or has a clearance, that suggests that his/her ability to safeguard classified information may be impaired or that his or her access to classified information may not be in the interest of national security. Cleared personnel should have a means to report adverse information regarding themselves or another cleared individual. The adverse information reporting should cover the 13 adjudicative topics identified earlier.

The reporting conditions currently published are what security professionals' term "insider threat indicators". Engage your company with an aggressive insider threat program that includes reporting and following through with a response to the activity. This closes a loop to ensure compliance with the National Industrial Security Program (NISP). One of the best applications is the continuous evaluation program.

After all, the cleared defense contractor is one entity in a chain that determines whether or not an employee requires a security clearance. Once the contractor submits a security clearance request, the employee is subject to a rigorous background investigation and adjudication process. If results are favorable, the employee is granted a security clearance.

So, why not continue this process throughout the cleared employee's career? Responsibilities don't stop with granted access. Throughout the employment, cleared employees are required to report any information that would lead to a decision that involved cleared employees which could become a security risk. This is called adverse information reporting. Cleared employees are required to report adverse information on themselves and other cleared employees. Failure to report could be discovered during the review.

Why the increased but redundant insider threat reporting requirement? You might recall the earlier reports we provided about captured spies. Many reports provided an example of well-trained employees reporting anomalies in employee behavior. The reports describe cleared employees making unusual requests for classified information they did not have need to know to access. Those stories and experiences demonstrate that these trusted employees had displayed signs and habits related to their intent. Extra time at the copy machines, request for information on other projects, unauthorized collection of data on storage devices and bringing banned recording devices into classified areas provided indicators of malintent. These days, it should be well understood in the NISP community that employees help by reporting issues.

Continuous evaluation involves identifying reportable information. So, why not apply a degree of continuous evaluation to address any behaviors that would identify employee security risks or insider threats? If your company performs classified work with cleared employees, you are already aware of risks to classified information and those reporting requirements.

So, why go through the excruciating work of identifying classified and other sensitive, information, only to be unable to control what employees do with it? How does reporting help? Reportable information involves a long list of events that may be way too detailed or voluminous to memorize.

That's where NISPOM required training comes in. The required topics include training security awareness and insider threat training. With training, you learn the concepts. It's not so important to be able to recite the reportable incidents as it is to just understand what is reported. In other words, it's the impact of adverse information over the laundry list of reportable items.

The impact of not reporting has a potential cost to lives, program success and damage to national security. Breaking down the long list of reportable events into bite size portions or categories is one way of educating the work force. It's not necessary to remember each and every report criterion but understanding categorically or holistically what should be reported. The ITPWG can work to define the impact of insider threat and the failure to report the adverse information.

Focus on Holistic Indicators

For example, it's not necessary to remember the plethora of indicators of espionage. It's sufficient to know that unauthorized access can lead to espionage or attempts to gain authorized access in unauthorized conditions should cause a reporting trigger. Unauthorized access attempts or attempted unauthorized use of access is reportable. The impact or motivation is not that important at the reportable point. We don't need to know that Sue is motivated by ideology to steal classified information. We just need to know classified information is protected and only those with need to know and a security clearance should access it during normal business hours. Any attempts otherwise should be reported and investigated.

Additionally, if anything is missing from classified inventory or accountability, it should be reported. We don't need to know motivation or intent; we just need to report that someone had capability and intent; now we are tracking. This prevents the need to focus on extracurricular activities of, or snoop on employees. We just need to report anomalies that display characteristics opposite of those cleared employees should display.

The point is, cleared employees are required to report observations of information that violates any of the 13 adjudicative criteria. These are required to be reported according to NISPOM however, while they can be leveraged for the ITP, they should not be the entire focus of the ITP. Having a team actively researching all cleared employees extracurricular activity is a tedious task that may not produce any information. These actions may produce protests, and legal and ethical concerns.

Reducing risk to classified information and reporting anomalies with the classified information should be the focus of the cleared defense contractor's ITP. By focusing on the classified information and not the employee, the ITP will have a better capability to understand acts of espionage, sabotage and subversion.

Insider Threat Triggers

Once these events are triggered, they should be reported immediately. Such reporting is out of an enterprise's jurisdiction and should be submitted to the FBI. Failure to report such incidents can be immediately identified as secrets are leaked (espionage), programs are destroyed (sabotage) or government departments are compromised (subversion). Developing the ITP to focus on vulnerabilities to classified information will increase chances of identifying and reporting:

- unauthorized access attempts
- identified targets of exploitation

With reporting and analysis, the ITP should focus on events that could trigger an insider threat concern. The reports should focus on employee behavior as it manifests from resources (employee movement behavior, security, HR, safety) and not on active spying on employees' private lives to determine if they are conducting spy craft. In other words, you are not being asked to go through garbage cans, read social media posts, listen in on phone calls, or otherwise use old school or technical means to spy on your employees. That would be illegal, wrong, and unethical. Having said that, this is typical of how many are interpreting the guidance. ITP guidance should be interpreted to include legal and ethical input as it applies to reporting observable behavior as it manifests in the workplace; not doggedly follow employees, looking for occasion.

While running the ITPWG, the ITPSO may not discover potential foreign intelligence attempts to gain access to a willing cleared employee. However, they may discover anomalies in employee work behavior as a result of recruitment such as unusual requests or demands. This could manifest in requesting access to information or areas without clearance or need to know, trying to badge into work during non duty hours without authorization, etc. A diligent employee may desire to report recruiting activities when approached and should be able to access a viable reporting avenue. Where an employee bent on espionage will not report and may quietly agree to provide espionage services, the ITP will most likely not have the tools or resources to discover recruiting attempts or agreements made in private. They will however be able to recognize anomalies in the recruited individual's activity. The ITPWG should filter and prioritize this information.

Unusual or unauthorized requests for classified information, increase in employee questions outside of work scope and unusual increase in requests for access to classified information beyond what they normally need are reportable activities are powerful red flags. On the other hand, reporting financial difficulties or alcohol use may be required, but the reporting itself may not lead to any insider threat issues. However, by analyzing reportable information, accountability and need to know issues the ITP can work to identify threatening behavior.

So, how does this work? The ITPWG should identify insider threat response actions to report incidents, investigate facts and refer to the proper authorities. There are laws and regulations limiting gathering, retention and use of data. That's why it's extremely important to include legal and ethical council. The ITPSO should understand and lead the ITPWG through the consequences of misusing information and impact of privacy laws and regulation.

A benefit of reporting is that the observer is relieved of the burden of action. With reporting, the trained employees should understand that they are removing themselves from the equation and letting others with the proper training, skills and appointment intercede. The employees should be trained that reporting is a positive action and they can permit themselves to report and remove themselves from the situation, investigation and jurisdiction.

Reported information should be discussed by the ITPWG and decisions made on how to move forward with necessary actions. In the case of classified information risks, reporting, potential classification spillage and impact to classified information is handled by the FSO. The ITPWG should weigh in with what to do about the reported information and preventing future instances. They should also revisit the risk assessment with the new incident to determine an updated risk and necessary mitigations.

Reporting Actions

The ITPSO should consider reporting from two points of view. The FSO is responsible for NISPOM required reports as discussed earlier. These reports should be part of the information the ITPWG will consider while working the ITP. However, some analysis may warrant additional reporting. The ITPSO should facilitate employee reporting required under NISPOM as well as how to report processed reporting analysis which may require a new Insider Threat Program report. The ITPSO may need to forward these ITPWG generated reports to the proper authorities.

For example, the FSO may have reported about an employee who committed a security violation. This report comes in several phases from initial to final reports to DCSA. The FSO conducts the investigation and submits a final report that holds the employee culpable and disciplinary action required. This report is closed out with DCSA.

The report triggers an ITPWG where the report is reviewed. Additionally, the ITPWG investigates what the cleared employee has access to based on clearance and need to know. In the course of the ITPWG, they review badge card access reports, information system processing records and other employee tracking technology. They soon determine that he has been accessing areas outside of the normal scope of responsibilities. Even though he is not working on some projects, print logs demonstrate he is printing classified pages related to those projects. This leads the ITPSO to file a new initial report and begin a new investigation in light of new analysis. Additionally, the ITPWG recommends taking on new measures to enforce need to know.

While NIPSOM lists reportable information, most of it may not lead to insider threat issues. Arrests, alcohol or drug use, or sexual behavior may indicate an individual could be a candidate for coercion, it doesn't mean they are necessarily a high risk for spy activity. However, issues of foreign influence, misuse of technology or suspicious interaction with access to classified information may be worthy of aggressive investigation. These examples include:

- Requests for information outside of need to know
- Unauthorized use of classified information
- Repeated security violations
- Bringing recording devices into secure areas
- Relationships with any known saboteur, spy, traitor, anarchist, or any espionage or secret agent of a foreign nation

Requests for information outside of need to know.

Once we understand the work that is classified and how the classified information is stored, generated, transmitted or otherwise worked, it's important to limit the access by the clearance level and need to know. Those with access and need to know should be aware of who they can provide access to. If request for access comes from unauthorized persons and they keep following up, this should be reported. Request for information can include attempting to bypass security procedures.

Unauthorized use of classified information

Employees can have authorization to access information, but not full permission to do as they please. The FSO and leadership can assign permissions to access information and limit access according to the permissions. Violations of permissions can be reported as unauthorized access. Permissions can cover the following:

- Unauthorized reproduction
- Unauthorized removal/destruction
- Unauthorized transmission
- Over-riding read / write / edit settings on information systems

Repeated security violations

This may not necessarily indicate a spy in the ranks, but this behavior brings risk to the organization and definitely falls under the insider threat program. Repeated security violations are a risk to classified information and should be reported. Security violations include:

- Losing classified information under their control
- Refusing to protect classifying information as required
- Repeated security infractions or violations

Bringing recording devices into secure areas

Sometimes employees forget they have recording devices on their person as they access secure areas. The reason it should be reported is to establish repeated behavior, determine how well training works, see if any additional countermeasures should be taken, and determine risk to classified information. On the other hand, you might just have an insider threat incident. There is no excuse for a trained employee to carry recording devices into an area where classified information exists. It's irresponsible at its best, espionage at its worst and should be a very rare or never occurring event. Discovery of recording devices should be taken very seriously, reported and the ITPWG should have access to reported information, circumstances and actions when and where investigations permit. These recording device reportable events include:

- Cameras
- Communication devices in classified areas
- Suspected surveillance devices
- Smart watches or other recording devices

Relationships with any known saboteur, spy, traitor, anarchist, or any espionage or secret agent of a foreign nation. Chalk this one up for reportable event. This is information that should be investigated. Additionally, consider reviewing what interaction the individual has with classified information. Consider the information, where the information resides, interaction with the information (generate, copy, transmit) and determine if there were any incidents of missing information or security violations.

CHAPTER 11 INSIDER THREAT TRAINING

Insider Threat Programs should provide required information to enterprise employees so that they understand their roles and how to gather, integrate and report relevant information. As a result, any potential insider threat reportable information and actions should be recognizable for a reasonably trained employee to report.

The Insider Threat Awareness Training should be provided to all employees at the time they are on boarded (within 30 days) and before they are given access to sensitive information. Additionally, more specific Insider Threat Program training should be provided to anyone serving on the Insider Threat Program Working Group.

Since the DCSA and maybe other organizations or customers may inspect your program, one way to ensure compliance is to bring your employees up to speed on requirements and how to implement the program. Auditors and inspectors not only ask questions to the ITP, but they may also randomly quiz employees. In the past, the ITP could brief, self-certify and provide artifacts to inspectors that their programs were effective and on point.

However, representatives (program office or DCSA) could ask open ended questions to your employees to determine how effective the training is. If employees cannot answer fundamental questions, it may leave an impression otherwise. An ITPWG or ITPSO can establish a good program on paper and with all appropriate signatures, certificates and attestations. However, if the program does not get implemented and trained, it won't appear effective.

The following questions are from the Self Inspection Handbook for NISP Contractors, published by DCSA. If employees can answer the following questions, it's a good indicator that your Insider Threat

Training is effective:

1. When was your last security briefing?
2. What do you recall from that briefing?
3. Can you recall any of the following topics being addressed in briefings?
   - Risk Management
   - Job Specific Security Brief
   - Public Release
   - Safeguarding Responsibilities
   - Adverse Information
   - Cybersecurity
   - Counterintelligence Awareness
   - Insider Threat
4. What is an insider threat?
   - What are some indicators of insider threat behavior and who would you report this to?
   - Can you recall any methods used to recruit trusted insiders?

It is a good practice to build the training so that your employees can better implement as well as demonstrate compliance. While Insider Threat training is a NISPOM requirement, a good place to begin implementing this training is to integrate it into already existing training or already established required training that cleared employees are required to attend (Figure 2).

Cleared defense contractor organizations are required to train their cleared employees on the following topics. These can be individual training events or a convergence of all topics into one event. Any of which will be a good introduction for Insider Threat Training:

- Initial Security Briefings
- Controlled Unclassified Information (CUI)
- A threat awareness security briefing, including insider threat awareness
- A counterintelligence awareness

- An overview of the security classification system
- Derivative classification
- Employee reporting obligations and requirements, including insider threat
- Initial and annual refresher cybersecurity awareness training for all authorized IS users
- Security procedures and duties applicable to the employee's job
- Refresher training for cleared employees

While any of the above are appropriate, the Initial Security Briefing is a good place to begin introducing employees to Insider Threat Training. Since it is a preexisting requirement, Insider Threat topics can be easily introduced into the existing training prior to new employees being granted access to classified information. Initial Security Briefings should include these essential elements to reduce insider threat risk:

- Threat awareness
- Counterintelligence (CI) awareness
- Overview of the information security classification system
- Reporting obligations and requirements, including insider threat
- Cybersecurity training for all authorized information system users in accordance with CSA-provided guidance
- Security procedures and duties applicable to the employee's position requirements and consequences that may result from the unauthorized disclosure of classified information

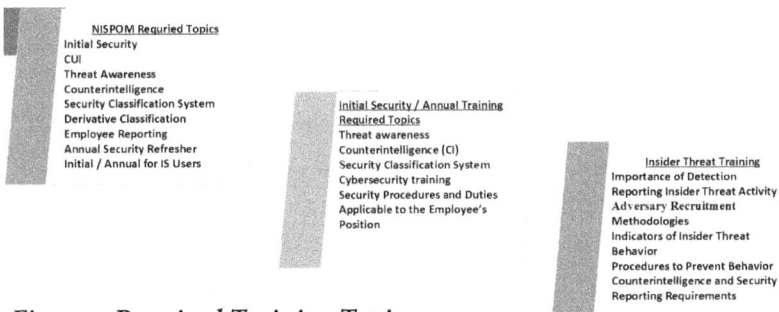

NISPOM Required Topics
Initial Security
CUI
Threat Awareness
Counterintelligence
Security Classification System
Derivative Classification
Employee Reporting
Annual Security Refresher
Initial / Annual for IS Users

Initial Security / Annual Training Required Topics
Threat awareness
Counterintelligence (CI)
Security Classification System
Cybersecurity training
Security Procedures and Duties
Applicable to the Employee's
Position

Insider Threat Training
Importance of Detection
Reporting Insider Threat Activity
Adversary Recruitment
Methodologies
Indicators of Insider Threat
Behavior
Procedures to Prevent Behavior
Counterintelligence and Security
Reporting Requirements

Figure 2 Required Training Topics

TRAINING TOPICS AND RECOMMENDED APPLICATION

Tell the employees what you will train them to do, conduct the training, and then tell them what you trained them to do. Finally, document the training. This is a proven methodology that assures a higher information retention rate. This will also help the employees better understand their roles and be better positioned to answer audit questions.

A more in-depth Insider Threat Training event should be developed as has its own curriculum specific to the task and provides employees with how to perform their ITP responsibilities. Required training topics for all employees will address current and potential threats in the work and personal environment and includes:

• The importance of detecting potential insider threats by cleared employees
• Reporting suspected activity
• Methodologies adversaries use to recruit trusted insiders and collect classified information, in particular within ISs
• Indicators of insider threat behavior and procedures to report such behavior
• Counterintelligence and security reporting requirements

The importance of detecting potential insider threats by cleared employees.
These topics should help employees understand the impact of losing sensitive information to an adversary. The impact should be easy to understand and effective. Some examples include:

• The system will fail to operate properly if sabotaged
• Competitors could acquire customers leading to loss of revenue and lay offs
• Adversaries could gain technology advantage bypassing their own research and development efforts
• Loss of contract due to competitor gaining knowledge of product development

Reporting suspected activity

Reporting an insider threat is a great mitigation strategy that can alert the appropriate ITP response. A credible report could lead to effective incident response to prevent damage to the organization or products.

Methodologies of adversaries to recruit trusted insiders and collect classified information, in particular within ISs

The training should include realistic methodologies that an adversary could use to get the cooperation of an inside employee. You may research industry appropriate examples and include case studies of strategies employed by adversaries or competitors. Realistic examples have great value in training.

Indicators of insider threat behavior, and procedures to report such behavior

Some information to incorporate into training is how to recognize potential insider threat behavior. In and of itself, most of the behavior may be innocent, but when compiled it could provide red flags. This is where it gets tricky, trying to balance harassing diligent employees with bad actors. Such best practice include reporting habits of good employees as:

- Working long hours
- Arriving early
- Staying late
- Making copies
- Asking detailed questions

Other more suspicious behavior may include:

- Changes in philosophy
- Expressing dissatisfaction with security procedures
- Lack of regard for policy
- Multiple security incidents
- Admiration of criminals
- Increased financial problems

- Sudden gain in wealth

Insider threat behavior is easier to recognize with technology to detect misuse of information systems such as:

- Attempting to bypass passwords
- Failed attempts to gain access to a network or computer
- Printing large amounts of paper copies
- Copying files on to removable media

Counterintelligence and security reporting requirements

The NISPOM has reporting requirements and the FSO should be managing that reporting channel. This should be incorporated into the organization's ITP. However, the ITPWG should address incident response and reporting for unclassified information that the organization includes in the ITP.

Those are the ITP requirements for all employees. Additionally, those serving on the ITPWG, require additional training to perform their designated duties. Employees with Insider Threat Program duties should be provided the following:

- Counterintelligence and security fundamentals
- Procedures for conducting insider threat response actions
- Applicable laws and regulations regarding the gathering, integration, retention, safeguarding, and use of records and data, including the consequences of misuse of such information
- Applicable legal, civil liberties, and privacy policies

Counterintelligence and security fundamentals.

This training topic will equip the ITPWG with fundamental knowledge on methodologies insiders or adversaries may use to exfiltrate sensitive information. It is up to the organization to acquire or develop the training for their employees. A good practice is to help the ITPWG understand the existence of the sensitive information, how it resides in the organization and how it could be accessed. Thoughts should be directed to developing and teaching effective countermeasures that deny, deter or detect insider threat activities.

Another method used to identify vulnerabilities is understand what the employees may discuss at any given time. It is important that employees limit discussion of sensitive information and do so in an approved area. Information that is an item, document, or on a computer may be easier to protect than information that a person could carelessly discuss. The spoken word provides an additional vulnerability. It is easier to establish policy to lock up and limit access to items than it is to prevent a person from freely discussing ideas in a Teams meeting or carpool discussion.

Protecting verbal communications requires training. Employees should understand and recognize information in their heads as sensitive and where they are authorized to discuss it. This should be included with insider threat training. The employee should understand what the information is, the sensitivity level, impact of unauthorized discussion, how to identify who to discuss with and where discussions are permitted. This can be documented as discussed earlier. The vulnerabilities occur where the person is involved. The information exists, it's in a person's thoughts, and is vulnerable where discussions are improper.

Some ways adversaries have used to access this type of information include elicitation and eavesdropping. Elicitation is a subtle form of questioning where conversation is directed to collect information. In its most basic use, an employee can reveal sensitive information in a conversation or during an interview or presentation. It is a different method than direct questioning and is harder to recognize. This can occur during a one-time opportunity, or as a long term recruiting method.

Eavesdropping is listening in on conversations to get information.

In this example, the outsider is taking advantage of overhearing conversations and gleaning valuable information. The insider is being careless or is intentionally revealing protected information for the benefit of the outsider. Some eavesdropping methods include electronic where the operator is using technology and equipment such as computers, directional microphone, bugging, and other items to gather sensitive information. Less technical means include reading lips and reading computer screens over an employee's shoulder. Finally, there are those that purposefully position themselves to overhear conversations, listen outside of meetings, or attend meetings under false pretenses

There are additional methodologies insiders and handlers can use to collect information. These include surveillance, theft, and interception of sensitive items and information. Surveillance is observation, studying work habits, developing target behaviors, developing plan to gain access from or trust of employees.

Procedures for conducting insider threat response actions
Incident response is a critical task and it is up to the ITPWG to determine incident response procedures. This training should engage the ITPWG to develop necessary processes that include a trigger from reportable actions, mitigations, and lessons learned.

Applicable laws and regulations regarding the gathering, integration, retention, safeguarding, and use of records and data, including the consequences of misuse of such information
This is a very important reason to involve legal, ethics, HR or other appropriate departments or consultants. Their input is key to managing an ITP that does not violate laws, regulations, and local policies. Ensure the training includes proper actions, legal practices and resolution if violations occur.

Applicable legal, civil liberties, and privacy policies
Another very important reason to involve legal, ethics, HR or other appropriate departments or consultants. Their input is key to

managing an ITP that does not violate laws, regulations, and local policies. Ensure the training includes proper actions, legal practices and resolution if violations occur.

Additionally, Insider Threat Training for the ITPWG should be developed, presented and documented. The ITPWG training focuses on providing very valuable information to the group responsible for the ITP success and passing reviews from oversight organizations such as DCSA.

When Insider Threat Training is conducted to standard, most employees should be able to answer the preceding questions confidently.

CHAPTER 12 NEXT STEPS

Now that you have learned what an insider threat is, how to develop a program, how to start an ITPWG and how to protect classified information from the insider threat, I recommend that you implement this book immediately. It's not necessary to begin everything at once, but start with an approach that is most effective, efficient and doable based on resources and requirements. This is a risk based solution, so make it relevant to risk.

The following appendices provide tools and templates to get you started. The appendices provide appointment letters, working group charters, training certificates and blank spreadsheets. Use the book to guide you and use the templates to document your progress. These templates should be presented during DCSA and other reviews.

While this book is most applicable to cleared defense contractors with classified information on site and multiple employees, it can be applied to non-possessing facilities as well as organizations with one to a handful of employees. For example, in all cases regardless of where classified work is performed and regardless of size of organization, an ITP is always required. The appointment memos and training are a must. Additionally, if a non-possessing organization, coordinate and loop in the ITP of the organization where employees actually perform classified tasks.

Make sure that while an ITPSO is directing the efforts that you include the senior management official and FSO (if not the ITPSO) in the implementation of your ITP.

Finally, I've developed other tools for you as well as additional books at our website. I hope you will visit to download ITP training and get additional resources.

I wish you the best of success as you *Establish an Insider Threat Program Under NISPOM.*

As you move forward, feel free to email me your thoughts, comments and recommendation. I am also available to help you establish your ITP.

APPENDICES

The following pages provide tools and templates to get you started with your ITP. The appendices provide appointment letters, working group charters, training certificates and blank spreadsheets. Use the book to guide you and use the templates to document your progress. These templates should be presented during DCSA and other reviews.

APPENDIX A - APPOINTMENT MEMO

Organization Name
Organization Address
Organization Phone Number

MEMORANDUM OF RECORD: Date:

Re: 32 Code of Federal Regulation (CFR) Part 117, NISPOM.
Senior Management Official Appointment

To Whom it May Concern:
___(Name)___, has been appointed as the Senior Management Official
(SMO) for CAGE _____ effective ___(Date)____.
___(Name)___ , is a U.S. citizen, cleared to the ___(Security Clearance
Level), granted ___(Date granted)___.
___(Name)___ has been briefed of their responsibilities in accordance with
Federal Register 32 CFR Part 117.

Respectfully,

___(Signature block)___

Organization Name
Organization Address
Organization Phone Number

MEMORANDUM OF RECORD:

Re: 32 Code of Federal Regulation (CFR) Part 117, NISPOM.
Facility Security Officer Appointment

To Whom it May Concern:
___(Name)___, has been appointed as the Facility Security Officer (FSO) for
CAGE _____ effective ___(Date)____.
___(Name)___ , is a U.S. citizen, cleared to the ___(Security Clearance
Level), granted ___(Date granted)___.
___(Name)___ has been briefed of their responsibilities in accordance with
Federal Register 32 CFR Part 117:

Respectfully,
___(Signature block)___

Organization Name
Organization Address
Organization Phone Number

MEMORANDUM OF RECORD:

Re: 32 Code of Federal Regulation (CFR) Part 117, NISPOM.
Insider Threat Program Senior Official Appointment

To Whom it May Concern:
___(Name)___, has been appointed as the Insider Threat Program Senior
Official (ITPSO) for CAGE _____ effective ___(Date)_____.
___(Name)___ , is a U.S. citizen, cleared to the ___(Security Clearance
Level), granted ___(Date granted)___.
___(Name)___ has been briefed of their responsibilities in accordance with
Federal Register 32 CFR Part 117:

Respectfully,
___(Signature block)___

Appendix B - Insider Threat Program Charter and Meeting Agenda

Organization Name
Organization Address
Organization Phone Number

MEMORANDUM OF RECORD: Date:

Insider Threat Program Charter

Re: 32 Code of Federal Regulation (CFR) Part 117, NISPOM.
Insider Threat Program Charter

___(Company name)___ has established an Insider Treat Program (ITP) as required by NISPOM. The ITP is formed pursuant to NISPOM and provided guidance to supplement unique mission requirements. Our ITP intent is to gather, integrate, and report relevant and available information indicative of a potential or actual insider threat, consistent with E.O. 13587 and Presidential Memorandum "National Insider Threat Policy and Minimum Standards for Executive Branch Insider Threat Programs."

The ITP is chartered and responsible for completing the following and documenting each task. The ITPSO will provide documentation upon request to demonstrate:

- Implementation of an Insider Threat Program (ITP) to deter and detect suspicious activities or threats (this memo serves as documentation)
- Designate a ITP Senior Official (ITPSO) (see appointment letter)
- Train the designated ITPSO, ITP group members and all cleared employees (see training certificates)

- Implement classified networks monitoring (if it exists)
- Maintain ITP records
- Conduct self-inspections of Insider Threat Programs (see results in Self-Inspection Handbook for NISP Contractors)

The success of the ITP is measured in methods to prevent unauthorized access of classified information, as well as protect sensitive information from malicious activities of a trusted insider with access and need to know. To do so, the ITPWG will focus on the following tasks and include them in ITP meeting agendas:

- Gather reportable information from resources and references
- Assess reportable information for impact to both the organization and classified information on-site
- Address reportable response to assessed risk
- Report insider threat occurrences
- Respond to insider threat incidents
- Identify sensitive information under the organization's control
- Identify vulnerabilities to sensitive information and items
- Identify and implementing information, system, cyber, physical security and appropriate disciplines to mitigate vulnerabilities
- Develop tailored guidance that employees can use to implement the countermeasures identified by the ITP
- Prepare, maintain, and update the ITP risk assessment elements in accordance with ITP requirements and schedules
- Continually evaluate the application of countermeasures and their effectiveness
- Document results and ITP efforts for DCSA or other review
- Brief ITP status to senior officials and stakeholders

The ITPWG will assign a note take to capture important comments, decisions, agenda items, assignments and accountability of tasks. The notes serve as a vehicle for moving forward and capturing decisions for historical value. The ITPWG decisions may successfully move forward or they could eventually be cancelled. However, as they move forward or resurrected with new contract requirements, the historical notes will play a valuable role in

consistency and rationale for decision making. For example, the ITPWG
may form to discuss the protection of a classified items as they go to test.
The discussion should focus on protection of the project during preparation,
transportation, storage, test result generation and messaging. The results
should ensure consistent protection according to marking and distribution
requirements, OPSEC considerations, and countermeasures.

The ITPWG meeting agendas will include the review of available security
classification guides, DD 254s, statements of work, and other relevant
documentation relating to classified information protection requirements.
The ITPWG will assess additional necessary protection and address
with enforced need to know and accountability measures. This ensures
consistency of protection.

The ITPSO has established an ITPWG to implement the ITP organization
wide. As a minimum, the following positions will always be part of the
ITPWG. Additional members will be appointed as necessary or as mission
dictates. They will be accounted for in meeting notes.

- Insider Threat Protection Official (ITPSO)
- Facility Security Officer

Respectfully,

___(Name)___
ITPSO
___(Signature block)___

MEMORANDUM OF RECORD: Date:

Insider Threat Program Charter Meeting Agenda

Re: 32 Code of Federal Regulation (CFR) Part 117, NISPOM.
Insider Threat Program Charter

The following agenda will be published for each ITPWG session. The ITPSO will ensure that all topics are covered as applicable and that notes are taken for a final meeting report to be signed by the Senior Management Official. This agenda will be published for each session and is intended to demonstrate compliance with the ITP guidance.

1. Opening comments

2. Review due outs from last meeting

3. Close out issues carried over from last meeting

4. Receive information from required sources

    a. Counterintelligence briefing if provided

    b. Threat assessment information if provided

    c. Security reports

d. Human Resources reports

e. List any additional reports acquired in meeting notes

5. Identify any actions to take as a result of reviewing reports. Actions taken should include analysis and measuring impact on classified information on location or at customer locations,

a. Crosswalk any reported employee activity with classified information the employee has access to

b. Review employee behavior monitoring:
- Access control
- Alarm reports
- Information management system audits

c. Determine if further reporting is necessary

d. Determine any risk or classified information internal or external to the organization

e. Identify any additional reports necessary as a result of analysis

6. Identify due outs and assign responsibility for follow-up

7. Identify any follow-up or coordination necessary with external ITPWGs

8. Closing comments or actions

Appendix C - Classified Information Inventory Management and Risk Matrix

Sensitive Item Name / PM or Project Lead	How sensitive item manifests (End item, Hardcopy, Softcopy, Software)	How sensitive item is marked (Classified, CUI, Export Controlled Organizational Markings)	Mandated Protection	Insider Threat Vulnerabilities	Insider Threat Countermeasures

CERTIFICATE OF TRAINING

THIS CERTIFIES THAT (EMPLOYEE NAME)

Has successfully completed:

Insider Threat Program Training

(DATE)

_____
ITPSO

_____
Senior Management Official

CERTIFICATE OF TRAINING

THIS CERTIFIES THAT (EMPLOYEE NAME)

Has successfully completed:

Insider Threat Training

(DATE)

_____
ITPSO

_____
Senior Management Official

About the Author

Jeffrey W. Bennett, ISOC, ISP®, SAPPC, SFPC is a system security engineer and security expert with experience in the Army, U.S. Government and as a Facility Security Officer (FSO). He consults full time with his other company, Thrive Analysis Group, Inc at https://www.thriveanalysis.com.

Jeff is enthusiastic about protecting our nation's secrets. He believes that integrity, influence and credibility are paramount qualities required of security professionals. His primary goal is to facilitate strong technology protection and NISP compliance. He is also a graduate of the FBI Citizen's Academy.

He's written many books and has training available on how to protect controlled technical information such as ITAR, CUI and classified information. Consider listening to his Podcast, DOD Secure.

Speaking Engagements

Jeff is available for speaking engagements. Contact him at jb@thriveanalysis.com for any of the following topics:

- Security Compliance
- Identifying and protecting:
  - ITAR
  - Controlled Unclassified Information (CUI)
  - Controlled Technical Information (CTI)
  - Classified Information
- Performing program protection requirements
- Leveraging policy to demonstrate compliance
- Establishing CUI Programs
- Establishing Insider Threat Programs
- Information Security
- OPSEC Planning
- Insider Threat Programs
- Enforcing Need to Know

On-Site Training:

Jeff is available to conduct on-site SPeD and ISP certification training. Additionally, Jeff is available to conduct the following training:

- FSO Certification
- NISPOM
- Program Protection Plan
- OPSEC
- Insider Threat Plan

Contact Jeff:
editor@redbikepublishing.com
Hear Jeff's Podcast at:
https://www.Nispomcentral.com

Red Bike Publishing

Our company is registered as a government contractor company with the CCR and VetBiz (DUNS 826859691). We are a Service Disabled Veteran Owned Small Business. Red Bike Publishing provides high quality books and training at:
www.redbikepublishing.com.

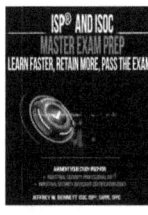

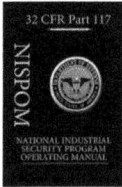

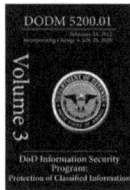

Books

This book, other security and NISP books and training are also available at our website. Helpful books include those part of the Security Clearances and Cleared Defense Contractor series by Red Bike Publishing:

- Insider's Guide to Security Clearances
- How to Get U.S. Government Contracts and Classified Work
- National Industrial Security Program Operating Manual (NISPOM)
- Self Inspection Guidebook for NISP Contractors
- International Traffic In Arms Regulation (ITAR)

Training

We provide NISPOM required cleared employee training that you can download and present. Topics include the following:

- SF-312 Non Disclosure Briefing
- Insider Threat Training
- Derivative Classifier Training
- Security Awareness Training

Find training at https://www.nispomcentral.com

NISPOM Fundamentals Course-Training that discusses each chapter of the NISPOM in depth; more than 15 hours of recorded training.

A Special Word of Thanks

Thank you for buying my book. I really appreciate you being a reader and hope you find it helpful. If you have any questions, please feel free to contact me.

I would really love to hear your feedback and your input would help to make the next version of this book and my future books better. Please leave a helpful review, where you purchased your book, of what you thought of it.

I would also ask that you let a friend know about the book as well. Thanks so much and best of success to you!!

Jeffrey W. Bennett

Sign up for our reader newsletter:
https://www.nispomcentral.com

www.ingramcontent.com/pod-product-compliance
Lightning Source LLC
Chambersburg PA
CBHW071748270326
41928CB00013B/2841